A HISTORY OF SPORT IN WALES

A POCKET GUIDE

A HISTORY OF SPORT IN WALES

MARTIN JOHNES

UNIVERSITY OF WALES PRESS
CARDIFF
2005

British Library Cataloguing-in-Publication Data
A catalogue record for this book is available from the British Library

ISBN 0-7083-1946-7

Printed in Malta by Gutenberg Press, Tarxien

Contents

Abbreviations

AFC	Association Football Club
BBC	British Broadcasting Corporation
CC	Cricket Club
CCC	County Cricket Club
FA	Football Assocation
FAW	Football Association of Wales
FC	Football Club
RFC	Rugby Football Club
WFU	Welsh [Rugby] Football Union
WRU	Welsh Rugby Union

Preface

> I find it rather absurd now to admit how much I enjoyed
> playing football. I gained pleasure from playing rugby or cricket
> or tennis or squash – but soccer was something else. That season,
> 1943-4, when I played for King's first eleven along with three
> other medical students I enjoyed my soccer more than ever
> before. I can remember the details of some games with disturbing
> clarity. I am sure it sounds kinky, and I have never thought of
> myself as kinky, but I enjoyed my soccer then, at least on some
> days, as much as I have sexual intercourse with the right person.
>
> Dannie Abse, *A Poet in the Family* (London, 1974), pp. 85–6.

Above all, sport is about fun. This was as true in 1800 as it was
in 2000. It has offered men, women and children a source of
physical, emotional and social satisfaction. Yet despite this
continuity, sport has undergone profound changes in the last
200 years. The character and structure of sport can only be
understood by locating it within the wider social, political and
economic context that shaped it. This book explores the
history of sport in Wales within this context. It is thus not a
history of great players and great matches but rather a social
history of an important part of Welsh culture.

The first chapter explores sport and games during the
emergent phase of industrialization that Wales experienced in
the early and mid nineteenth century. It shows how wider
social and economic change was key to laying the foundations
of modern sport. Chapter two looks at the emergence of
modern organized sport in the late Victorian and Edwardian
periods. It explores the role immigration played in introducing
new sports to Wales and argues that sport played a key part in
binding together the new industrial communities and forging

a wider popular sense of Welsh nationhood. Yet sport was also socially divided and could provide individuals with a means of signifying their status and excluding social inferiors. Chapter three looks at sport from the 1920s to the 1950s. It shows that although sport was already heavily commercialized there was also a thriving culture of actually playing. Chapter four explores sport from the late 1950s to the present day, an era in which professional sport came to be dominated by the needs and concerns of television and commerce. The conclusion reiterates some of the book's key themes and offers some final thoughts on the relationship between sport and national identity in Wales. This book sets out to introduce readers to ideas and themes prevalent within academic sports history and it thus finishes with a guide to further reading.

As in any book, the coverage here is selective. Events, individuals and processes have been chosen according to their perceived importance or role in illustrating a wider point or trend. Thus some individuals and sports, especially rugby and football, are probably over represented, whilst others do not get the coverage that some might feel they deserve. The book's coverage is also influenced by the work and research that has gone before it. The study of the social history of sport may have grown in the last twenty years but there are still significant gaps in our knowledge. Beyond boxing, there has been little written about individual sports in Wales. Women's involvement in sport, whether as players or spectators, is a particularly under-studied arena and until it develops survey books such as this one will remain dominated by men's team games. Studies of nearly every aspect of Welsh society are somewhat dominated by the industrial south and this book is no different. West, mid and north Wales are, of course, explored but there remains much scope for further research on sport in rural Wales and the nation's more peripheral industrial districts.

Like any book, this work has been completed with the direct and indirect help of many people. Colleagues in the British Society of Sports History have provided a critical and stimulating wider audience for my ideas. Students at St Martin's have further helped sharpen and question my ideas and generally forgiven the prominence of Welsh examples in their seminars and lectures. Anthony Beer, Tim Barry, David Bond, Patrick

Chaplin, Jon Cryer, Alun Evans, Ian Gavin, Chris Johnes, Bill Jones, Paul O'Leary, Matthew Taylor, Hamish Telfer, Jonathan Thomas and Amanda West have all supplied or helped locate various sources. I am especially grateful to Andy Croll, John Harris, Emma Lile, Mike Huggins, Chris Williams and Gareth Williams who read and commented on drafts of various chapters.

The faculty of Arts, Humanities and Social Sciences at St Martin's College, Lancaster, kindly provided financial assistance for research trips back to Wales thus making this book possible. My wife Heather Moyes continues to put up with my obsessions and support me in every way possible. Finally, my daughter Bethan turned up near the completion of the book and has already shown great promise by learning to cheer when told that Swansea have scored.

Martin Johnes
Summer 2005

1

Industrialization and the Origins of Modern Sport, 1800–1880

At the time of the 1801 census, Wales was home to 587,345 people. Merthyr Tydfil, Wales's largest town, had just 7,705 inhabitants but was surrounded by iron forges, fired by coal from the small workings that were scattered across south Wales. Merthyr was a sign of Wales's industrial future but it was from agriculture that the vast majority of people scratched their living at the start of the nineteenth century. In both town and country, life was not easy for the masses: work was long and dangerous, while housing was dark, overcrowded and unhealthy. Infant mortality in 1850s Merthyr was a terrifying 18.4 per cent. In such a harsh environment, recreation took on an added importance.

I

The sports and games of pre- and early industrial Wales were not clearly demarcated activities but rather part of a communal festive culture that saw people congregate to celebrate high days and holidays and eat, drink, gamble and play. The sports of the people reflected their lives: they were rough, proud and highly localized. Rules were unwritten and based on customs and informal agreements that varied from place to place according to local oral traditions. Football had been popular across England and Wales since at least medieval times, but its exact form was highly localized and resembled a mass mêlée more than its modern descendant. In 1603 George Owen gave a vivid description of a primitive version of football called *cnapan* in Pembrokeshire. He revealed a complex pastime with 'great multitudes' of spectators and rules governing the violence and use of horses.[1] Later Welsh forms of what historians have called 'folk' football do not seem to have either shared the title of *cnapan* or its horseback players. They did however continue to have teams that were only rarely limited to precise numbers but which were united by ties of blood or community. Games could last from noon until dusk, goals were landmarks that varied from church porches to rivers, while the field of play might be the streets of a country town or several miles of open countryside. The games' communal nature reflected a rural society where people depended upon each other to help gather the harvest and survive in times of distress. The dates on which this folk football was played fitted in with the rural calendar: holidays and harvests when people came together to celebrate. The contests were the subject of much local pride and were keenly fought, as one old player remembered: a man 'would as soon lose a cow from his cow-house, as the football from his portion of the parish'.[2] It was said that in south Cardiganshire 'the population, rich and poor, male and female, of opposing parishes, turned out on Christmas Day and indulged in the game of football with such vigour that it became little short of a serious fight'.[3] Victories and losses sank into local folklore, to be celebrated and lamented, repeated and avenged.

While Christmas and Shrove Tuesday were common dates for football, so too were the festivals of local parish patron saints known as *gwylmabsantau* in Wales and wakes in England. The *gwylmabsantau* were the occasion for communal feasts, followed by racing and fighting amongst people and animals, ball games and tests of strength, such as throwing the bar or lifting a stone, as well as plenty of drinking and dancing. The celebrations crossed class boundaries and were enjoyed by both sexes and all ages but the exact form varied from parish to parish and such festivals were symbolic representations of the pride and autonomy of individual parishes and the differentiation between them.[4] Across Britain, other significant local events could also be the subject for such games and sports. At Llawr-y-Gors near Pwllheli in 1853 a 'rural sports' day was held to celebrate the birthday of the heir to a local estate. The day included donkey races, sack races, catching greasy-tailed pigs, wheelbarrow races blindfolded and the climbing of a greasy pole.[5] Within this festive culture, sports were not as neatly defined as in later days. At Oswestry in the 1820s contestants at a sports day had to be the quickest to consume sticky buns hanging from a rope.[6] Of course, people also played sports and games outside the special festivals. Fives was a primitive version of squash that involved bouncing a ball off a wall with one's hands. In 1811 it was said to be almost 'a national pursuit, in which both boys and men very generally and eagerly engage'.[7] Churchyards were a favourite venue, if only because few other places had accessible and large stone walls. Despite the sacred surroundings, markings were made on the church walls and games contested for money and ale. So ingrained were churchyards as venues for local games that some churches even had niches for the prize ale that parsons gave to the winners of contests.[8]

Bando or bandy was the first mass spectator sport in modern south Wales.[9] It was a crude version of hockey that involved hitting a ball along the ground with a curved stick. The sport was especially popular on the south Wales coast, with known venues including the beaches at Baglan and Aberavon. The rules were localized but regulated to enable gambling and a degree of order in contests that produced a 'heartburning' rivalry and 'jealousy' between parishes. Driven by such patriotisms, games attracted crowds as large as 3,000, who were kept lubricated by beer from enterprising brewers. Teams tended to consist of between twenty and thirty players but 'multitudes of spectators and partisans, too, often mingle[d] in the contest'.[10] Pedestrianism, an eclectic early form of athletics that took advantage of the improving roads of the nineteenth century, was another sport that attracted spectators in the early and mid-nineteenth century. Some races were tests of endurance over huge distances; others were simple running races. William Gale of Cardiff was said to have walked 2,232 miles in 1,786 consecutive half hours. Like many of his contemporaries, he was accused of cheating by using a substitute during the hours of darkness.[11] The stakes, prizes and challenges varied from pride to beer to cash, but betting was a constant feature in a sport that produced professional racers who were popular heroes with reputations and experience that extended into England. John Davies, nicknamed *Y Cyw Cloff* (the lame chick), was born near Bridgend in 1822 and could run a mile in less than five minutes. His glories were celebrated in popular local ballads: 'The noisy English are forever bragging their intentions of defeating the Welsh, but Morgan's land has got one who can beat the lot'. He took advantage of his fame and later ran an inn near Pontypridd.[12] Publicans searching for additional trade organized many of the races with their inns acting as starting and finishing points and focal venues for the thirsty spectators that could number in their thousands. Thus even in its pre-modern forms, sport was neither free from commercial motives nor the disputes that betting, prizes and rules brought.

If pedestrianism was a sport that signalled future developments, blood sports were pastimes rooted in the past. Dog and cock fighting, bull and badger baiting (where the animal was tied to a post and set upon by dogs) and rat killing *en masse* were sports known to the Welsh of all classes. The natural aggression of cocks was supplemented by attaching sharp spurs to their feet, while special pits and rings were built to allow crowds to watch the slaughter. Throwing at cocks was a particularly brutal pastime whereby the bird was tethered and then stoned to death, with the thrower of the fatal stone keeping the carcass. There was a commercial element to such sports: gambling was common and in Wrexham people paid a fee to enter their dogs into the weekly bull bait. The sums involved could be quite substantial. An 1818 fight between the cockerels of 'gentlemen from Montgomeryshire and Flintshire' had a top prize of 100 guineas.[13] Rural societies saw animals as resources that existed to be utilized by man, whether for his sustenance, service or enjoyment. Thus those who took part by no means thought the sports barbaric. Given that slavery was not abolished in the British Empire until 1833, a lack of compassion for animals is perhaps not surprising.

II

Yet taking delight in the pain of animals was beyond the pale of middle-class respectability in a society that increasingly thought itself civilized and enlightened, and by the turn of the nineteenth century blood sports were under attack from middle-class moralizers. In 1822 some publicans in Kenfig only held their licences on condition that the premises were not used for 'cockfighting and the baiting of bulls, bears and badgers'.[14] However, it was not until the 1835 Cruelty to Animals Act that there was a legislative underpinning to the campaigning of animal protectionists. Even amongst its strongest proponents, animal protection could be as much about suppressing dangerous and deviant human behaviour as protecting animals. In 1827 bull baiting was banned in the market town of Llantrisant, not because of its cruelty but because it attracted unruly crowds. The campaigns of the Society for the Prevention of Cruelty to Animals were firmly aimed at the working classes, who often received less compassion from their social superiors than animals did.[15] The abuse of animals by the gentry and upper classes remained very much unchecked.

The opposition to blood sports was largely secular but religious bodies were influential in attacking traditional games and sports. Methodists and other Nonconformist groups, who began to dominate Welsh religion in the late eighteenth century, were particularly active in preaching against sports and appropriating the holidays on which they were played. Folk football was already in severe decline across Britain by the nineteenth century but continued to be the subject of religious attacks. In Llanwenog, near Lampeter, the annual Christmas Day football match ended in the 1830s when 'a venerable Nonconformist minister preached against it, and the people listened to him'.[16] In Cardiganshire, a riotous football match, known as *Y Bêl Ddu* (the black ball) and played between two parishes every New Year's Day, was deliberately supplanted in 1833 with a scriptural competition between Sunday schools.[17] Nonconformists also attacked the *gwylmabsantau*, and although they were still in evidence at the end of the nineteenth century in Nonconformist strongholds such as Anglesey, the festivals mostly fell away in the 1830s and 1840s.[18] Of course, people would not simply follow the wishes of preachers if they did not at least partly sympathize with the cause, and Nonconformity enjoyed a popular and sometimes fanatical following amongst the Welsh working class. Chapels were built in Wales at a rate of one every eight days in the first half of the nineteenth century.[19] A description of Caernarfonshire, written in 1811, noted, 'of these fooleries and pastimes the greater part now lie buried in the grave dug for them partly perhaps by the growing intelligence of the people, but certainly with a more immediate effect by the sour spirit of Methodism'.[20] Another writer noted in 1802 that the 'sudden decline' of the

> Customs of Wales, is in a great degree to be attributed to the fanatick imposters, or illiterate plebian preachers, who have too often been suffered to over-run the country, misleading the greater part of the common people from their lawful Church; and dissuading them from their innocent amusements, such as Singing, Dancing, and other rural Sports, and Games, . . . the consequence is, Wales, which was formerly one of the merriest, and happiest countries in the World, is now become of the dullest.[21]

Although such marginalized Anglicans frequently blamed the religious dissenters for social ills, the Established Church was itself not above using the spectre of hell to discourage local games. An inscription on a churchyard wall at Llanfair Discoed near Caerwent read 'Whoever hear on Sunday, Will practis playing at Ball, It may be before Monday, The Devil will have you all'.[22] In England too, where Nonconformity was much weaker, traditional games also declined at this time. The opposition to sports in churchyards probably owed much to the more profane destruction of windows by errant balls.[23] In the Vale of Clwyd Victorian church restorations removed ball courts from churchyards and filled spaces previously used for games and dances with huge marble graves.[24]

Practical and political fears also underpinned attacks on football and pedestrianism. The first half of the nineteenth century was a period of social unrest, as the rural and urban poor reacted against economic hardships and the inequalities of society. The early and mid nineteenth century witnessed periodic food riots, vigilante action against those who abused popular notions of legitimate moral and economic behaviour, and, most famously, the destruction of exorbitant toll gates by Rebecca's Daughters. In Newport in 1839 there was even an armed rising that may have been intended as the starting point of a Chartist revolution to bring a workingmen's democracy. Eight years earlier, the red flag had been hoisted during an armed rising in Merthyr that brought the intervention of troops and left sixteen dead. Such tensions were underpinned by demographic changes that seemed to suggest things would only get worse. The population of Wales doubled in the first fifty years of the nineteenth century and was increasingly skewed towards the south. By 1872, 42 per cent of the Welsh population lived in Glamorgan and Monmouthshire, a proportion that had doubled since the turn of the century. The two counties were now amongst the most urbanized in Britain. The problem of an increasing number of hungry mouths was more threatening when they were concentrated in urban sprawls.

In such a context, the chaos and unruliness of folk football were unwelcome, especially when people took it into the towns. On Shrove Tuesday in Laugharne in Carmarthenshire, teams 'contested with no small degree of energy and violence who should impel the ball first to an appointed goal at either end of town'. In 1838, the local magistrates, seeing the game as a public nuisance, suppressed it and had the two ringleaders hauled before them.[25] Concerns about the rowdy and immoral behaviour of the working classes pushed pedestrianism, with its gambling, cheating, and drunk and rowdy spectators, to the boundaries of urban life, while encouraging, with the help of the new police forces, prosecutions for technicalities like obstruction. Furthermore, a popular culture that was riotous and unruly was also at odds with the regular hours demanded by industry. In 1815, the *Cambrian* newspaper complained:

> What was before the disease of an individual has now become an epidemic; and where it will end I know not. Already several masters of numerous workmen assure me that they can scarcely keep them to business, and that all ambition has forsook them except that of going over a certain length of ground within a certain time . . . The rage prevails, and those who in our workshops and manufactories were known as *good hands*, are now only desirous of proving that they have *good legs*.[26]

Such attacks reduced the regional diversity of sports and games in Wales. This was part of a wider move across Britain towards a more homogeneous culture, as railways made the nation appear smaller, industrialization changed the social and physical face of the land and the abolition of the old localized poor laws gave parishes less autonomy and individual character. Indeed, these wider changes were as important in bringing the decline of traditional localized games and customs as the religious and political attacks upon them.

Prizefighting (bareknuckle boxing) was another professional sport that incurred the wrath of the authorities and was condemned not just for its violence per se but also because of the fear that it would encourage working-class men to resort to violence in the home and workplace. In 1885 the *Aberdare Times* declared the pastime an 'outrage to decency'.[27] As a result, it was marginalized to 'bloody spots' on mountainsides or the back streets of towns where it could escape the disapproving eyes of the law and ministers but still be enjoyed by crowds of onlookers. Nonetheless, it was regulated by rules and conventions, if only to lessen the opportunities for corruption over the frequent and heavy betting on fights. The sport's leading practitioners were popular heroes who fought for money as well as pride and fame. One such boxer was Dan Bach Pontypridd, who was born in 1823 and ran a pub in Cardiff. He went on to defeat English and American champions and to be celebrated in popular ballads. When Dan Bach was an old man, future champion Freddie Welsh asked for his advice, only to be told, 'give it up, it doesn't pay'.[28] Prizefighting was especially popular in the booming iron districts that centred on Merthyr and Dowlais. Thanks to the success of the industry, 150,000 people lived in the eighteen miles between Hirwaun and Blaenavon in the 1840s, making it the most concentrated and important iron-producing district in the world. Here living conditions were especially harsh, overcrowded and unhealthy. The endemic crime, violence and drunkenness offered means of survival as well as entertainment. Stealing enabled some to eat and fighting enabled others to win much-needed money or to impose their authority on weaker souls around them. Prizefighting was thus in tune with the rhythms of life in the iron district.

The urban heartland of the iron towns both horrified and frightened middle-class observers. The suppression of traditional activities, both in and out of towns, not only displayed an authoritarian attitude towards the working classes, it also demonstrated a lack of understanding of their culture. This was true across Britain but in Wales it was complicated by the fact that most of the interior life of the masses was conducted through the Welsh language. Yet religious, social and legal attacks did not completely destroy the traditional popular culture of Wales, even within urban areas.[29] The persuasion of peers and the wider community could bring back a converted Methodist to his previous predilection for games.[30] Football was noted in Dolgellau in 1850 and in the rural market town of Narberth as late as 1884, where on Shrove Tuesday 'all the shutters are put up, and the principal thoroughfare is given over to the players'.[31] Most continuing games of football however were probably much smaller and less ritualized than their festive ancestors. In 1871, Francis Kilvert, a curate in the parish of Clyro in the Wye valley, Radnorshire, observed that after the parish Harvest festival dinner, 'all the men played or rather kicked football at each other and then till it grew dark, when the game ended in a general royal scuffle and scrummage'.[32] The sports days associated with the *gwylmabsantau* continued past the decline of the festivals themselves. They did however gain a commercial bent, as publicans and other entrepreneurs took up their organization in search of profits. The 1851 Whit Monday 'usual Rustic Sports' at Crymlyn Burrows were advertised to 'holiday-folks of Swansea, Neath etc' via an announcement in the press that promised 'wrestling, leaping, jump in sacks, shooting for a good pig, boys running for a splendid hat, a running match between Swansea and Neath ladies, for a pound of "real souchong", and a race to run by "sporting boys" above 60 years of age'.[33] Here, sport existed as part of a wider culture of merriment, with its roots in the past but with a distinctly commercial edge.

Poaching, which boasted many sporting qualities thanks to the stealth and skill required and the friction caused by the employment of English gamekeepers, was another activity that the authorities tried to banish. Supporting and enforcing laws protecting even common quarry such as rabbits was a way for the gentry to assert their social status and privilege in the face of wider change and upheaval. It was also, of course, a way of protecting the field sports that played an important role in filling their long hours of leisure. There was a widespread feeling amongst many members of the rural working classes that poaching was a perfectly legitimate activity and it was common for poachers to appeal to the 'immemorial rights' of locals to take game and fish from particular locations, or even from the entire countryside.[34] Even magistrates sometimes shared such sympathies. A letter in the English press complained that in Welsh courts 'it is not the exception for poachers to get off scot free, nor to be fined a nominal sum for the sake of appearances. For this reason many parishes are nearly, if not quite, destitute of game'.[35] When popular and establishment definitions of legitimacy varied so significantly,[36] it was not surprising that many traditional activities survived the attempts to stamp them out.

III

In the process of its hunting and, increasingly in the second half of the nineteenth century, its shooting, the gentry and aristocracy butchered large numbers of animals and birds. In 1885 a shooting party on a Merioneth estate killed 5,086 rabbits in a single day.[37] Yet the gentry largely escaped the wrath of the Society for Prevention of Cruelty to Animals because of their social status. This was not just because it was more difficult to prosecute and persecute the gentry but also because they were seen as being more able to contain their cruelty towards animals. Whether an act was seen as vice or virtue could be a matter of who exactly the saint or sinner was. Indeed, fox hunting was even portrayed as providing a useful service to local tenant farmers. In the face of present social and political unrest, the memory of the French Revolution was both potent and lingering and the aristocracy could not afford to be seen as too indulgent and rooted in pomp and circumstance. Thus the aristocracy's need to prove itself tough and useful to both its tenants and to the country at large was influential in boosting the popularity of fox hunting across Britain.[38] So too was its ability to bond this rural elite by bringing together 'parts of the county members who would not otherwise meet'.[39] Running a private pack and providing the dinners that were essential to a good day's hunt required wealth, and hunting was thus also a way of actually signalling one's position in society. As the wealth and status of the aristocracy steadily declined through the nineteenth century, some of the traditional hunting packs suffered financial hardships because of the problems of their patrons. However, when the snobbery and financial needs of the local hunt consented, there was 'new money', as well as those of more limited means, who were happy to take up foxhunting in search of the thrill of the chase and the associated social cachet. Subscribers to the Rhondda hunt included miners, while in Pembrokeshire they included tenant farmers.[40] Other working-class participation simply took the form of watching or following the grand spectacle of the huntsmen in order to brighten up what were otherwise often dull and hard lives.[41] Thus, despite its exclusivity, in 1840 foxhunting was said by Montgomeryshire hunters to have 'a direct tendency to promote Unanimity, Sociality and Kind Feeling among all classes of Society and is a truly British sport'.[42]

Hunting ensured that horses were an important part of the culture of the British gentry and aristocracy. In 1872 Monmouthshire became home to the first provincial polo club in Britain,[43] but it was horse racing that was possibly the most organized of all pre-modern sports. By 1833 the governing *Racing Calendar* recognized flat races at Cowbridge, Haverfordwest, Conwy, Aberystwyth, Brecon, Carmarthen, Knighton and Wrexham. The prestigious Cowbridge races attracted entries from as far away as Yorkshire but were dominated by the local gentry who used them as a social gathering as much as a place to test their prized horses. All races were the scenes of heavy betting and associated entertainments that varied from exclusive balls and dinners to pig races. The peripheral side-shows, the unenclosed nature of the courses and the general excitement of the day attracted less desirable sorts such as drunks, prostitutes and pickpockets, as well as a horde of ordinary men and women. This made racing a place where the classes met but it remained very much under the control of the landed gentry. The races that were confined to the horses of tenant framers, such as those at the Pembroke steeplechase in 1870, were essentially token gestures in a gentleman's world. By offering his financial support to races, an ambitious gentleman could use racing to demonstrate 'his largesse and concern for local events'. There was money to be made by the selling and breeding of horses but this does not seem to have been a strong motive for the involvement of the gentry. Racing however was part of a wider British elite culture and was promoted in Wales for precisely this reason. Under pressure from Nonconformist radicals, because of the religious and linguistic barriers between them and their tenants, the Welsh gentry were keen to ingratiate themselves with their English, and even European, peers.[44] Racing itself could also come under religious pressure because of the unruly behaviour that accompanied it. A burial ground was desecrated and brass stolen from the tombs after the Wrexham races one year in the middle of the nineteenth century. After pressure from a local vicar the races were abandoned in 1862. They were resurrected in 1890 but then faced opposition from Nonconformists who complained that the races were 'a source of inhuman cruelty to dumb animals, and of untold demoralisation to the town and district'.[45]

Archery was another sport whose popularity owed something to the social and cultural needs of the upper classes. In the late eighteenth and early nineteenth century, in the face of industrialization and political uncertainty, there was an aristocratic fashion across Europe for nostalgic medievalism, a period when the social order had been secure and the world had been rural. Encouraged by this prevailing fashion and the patronage of members of the royal family, archery societies were set up across Britain, each with its own strict entry criteria, outlandish costumes and extravagant dinners. They were havens of exclusivity and good company, and thus a way of reinforcing and reassuring one's own position in society. Furthermore, women could not only compete in the contests but retain and display their 'feminine forms' whilst doing so, and thus the clubs also acted as a forum for flirtation and voyeurism.[46] In the Royal British Bowmen of Denbighshire, Wales could boast one of Britain's most prestigious and famous archery clubs, whose patrons included the Prince of Wales and the most prominent families in north-east Wales and Shropshire. The Bowmen toured around the country houses of the members, complete with their own marquee and servants. Members 'marched two and two to the shooting ground, the music playing a new march composed for the occasion, and colours flying. On their arrival at the ground, a royal salute of 21 guns was fired'. As seen in hunting, the aristocracy and gentry did not have bottomless pockets and the cost of hosting such picturesque extravagance meant that many members declined their turn to host the shoots.[47]

As the wealth of the aristocracy declined and fashion moved on, the character of archery changed. In the second half of the nineteenth century, archery found a new popularity with the provincial middle classes. This was clear in the diaries of Radnorshire curate Francis Kilvert who attended 'croquet and archery parties' and shot with friends on lawns and in meadows. With something of an eye for female beauty, he relished the opportunity that the two sports gave him for contact with attractive young women such as 'lovely little May Oliver with her bewitching face, beautiful dark eyes and golden curls. She was shooting and had no quiver, so I acted as quiver for her, holding her arrows, picking them up, and being her slave generally.'[48] Kilvert was also aware that the skill of the pretty archers was not always up to much:

> Margaret Oswald told me that as I put my head through the railings to rake a croquet ball out of the field on to the lawn, my head looked so tempting that she felt greatly inclined to shoot at it. Certainly there would have been this comfort that if she had shot at me I should have been very much safer than if she had not, because wherever else the arrow might have gone, it certainly would not have hit me.[49]

Archery and croquet were thus more like pastimes than conventional competitive sports and were part of a middle-class social scene that was centred on respectable interaction and gentle flirtation between the sexes.

The gentry were also at the forefront of cricket, which was, in many ways, the oldest of all modern sports played in Wales. Sets of rules emerged in eighteenth-century England in order to help settle arguments over the heavy wagers that were often made on the outcome of games. The Welsh gentry's adoption of cricket was another step in its anglicization. The first recorded cricket match in Wales (although almost certainly not the first to take place) was in 1783 at Court Henry Down, near Carmarthen between two teams of local gentlemen and clergy. By the first third of the nineteenth century, there were cricket clubs across the south of Wales, playing convivial matches against each other and teams from England. Wales's first county sides were Monmouth and Brecon, who played each other in 1825, but cricket enjoyed a following across Wales. Yet with travel difficult and expensive before the advent of railways, intra-club games, such as that held by Swansea Cricket Club in 1831 between married and single members, were more common. As with all the sports of the gentry, the social side of cricket was central to its popularity, and matches were accompanied by betting, drinking and lavish dinners. In the first half of the nineteenth century the game itself was somewhat crude. Over-arm bowling did not emerge until the 1860s, while the varying number of players on a team took to the field in tall hats with coloured and patterned jackets. The rough, uneven and some-times completely unprepared fields and meadows that were played on meant that games could be dangerous. In 1858, a Pontypool player died from a brain haemorrhage after being hit by a ball on the temple during a practice session.[50]

The gentry's desire to win the heavy wagers placed on games encouraged them to look for talented players outside their own elite circles. To the distaste of some observers, profession-alism thus crept into the sport as gentlemen employed talented players as groundsmen so they could play in the country house teams. By 1850, Cardiff Cricket Club had a professional adviser and instructor hired on a weekly basis. Other teams employed professionals on casual terms for one-off matches, particularly for derby games where pride was as important as the wagers. The building of railways across the country in the 1840s and 1850s enabled more regular games between clubs in and outside Wales. The opportunity to play alongside the gentry attracted the *nouveaux riches* and members of the professional classes. Tradesmen, too, began to play, forming their own teams where time or snobbery prevented them from joining the established teams. The 1850s and 1860s thus saw a large rise in the number of clubs, five of which, for example, were in Haverfordwest alone.[51] Because of the limited free time working men enjoyed, an Early Risers' cricket club was formed in Merthyr in 1848. The club practised three times a week at 5.30 in the morning.[52] The stationing of troops in Wales following the Rebecca riots and Chartist unrest of the late 1830s and early 1840s, further helped the development of cricket. Cricket fields were built for the new barracks and the soldiers provided regular opposition for local clubs. As one Monmouthshire newspaper noted, these games helped 'relieve body and mind from the severe toil and anxiety now felt by all classes during these eventful times'.[53] Cricket also found a place in the new schools created after the 1840 Grammar Schools Act, and old boys from these schools went on to set up teams in later life. The diffusion of the game owed something to the increasing paternalism of the local elite. The ironworks-owning Guest family of Dowlais, for example, provided a ground on which their workers could play and a tent. Yet despite the expanding social base of the game, it was still marred by wider social cleavages. The Montgomeryshire club (formed in 1855) limited membership to gentlemen, while Carmarthenshire refused trades-men as members.[54]

From the mid-1850s a touring England select team played regular matches against specially selected Welsh sides. The popularity and success of these games led to the formation of the South Wales Cricket Club in 1859, essentially a touring side of gentlemen, augmented by a few locals and profes-sionals. Amongst the guest players was W. G. Grace, who first played for the club as a fifteen-year-old in 1864. South Wales CC declined in the mid-1860s and was replaced by Cadoxton CC of Neath as the most important and influential Welsh team. In 1868, the club entertained a side of Australian abori-gines at St Helen's in Swansea, the first overseas touring side to visit Wales. The club's status was confirmed when it beat a MCC team at Lord's in 1869. As Hignell noted, the fixture indicated that cricket in south Wales had come of age.[55] When the South Wales club was resurrected in 1874, with a view to it providing a coordinating and organizing role for cricket in the region, a vote to exclude professionals from the club was defeated, a sign that sport, and maybe even Welsh society, was becoming more democratic.

IV

Cricket's growth in the 1850s to 1870s coincided with a period of greater social harmony in Wales and a new wave of industrialization that saw coal gradually replace iron as the underpinning economic *raison d'être* of south Wales and the valleys of the Rhondda begin their urban transformation. Learning from past tensions, industrialists began to be more paternal towards their workers, who increasingly lived in towns blessed with basic sanitation. Nonconformist ministers continued their quest to create a respectable and 'tidy' working class, particularly after the 1847 'treason of the blue books', a government report into education that branded Nonconformism and the Welsh language as responsible for an immoral and ignorant people. The increasing popularity of the Liberal Party was a partial response to such slander and gave Wales a radical reputation that united the working and middle classes. Most important however in bringing a degree of social harmony was the relief of some of the more overt economic hardships in industry and agriculture. There was, of course, not complete tranquillity. Riots and strikes still occasionally worried industrial and rural Wales, while overcrowding and poor sanitation quickly became problems in the coal districts. Nonetheless, the increased social and economic stability helped the emergence of the more organized sports that replaced the loss of the more obvious signs of traditional pastimes such as the *gwylmabsantau* and folk football.

Paternalism in industry and housing was paralleled in leisure by the spread of 'rational recreation'. The continued popularity of pubs and the crowds of onlookers that gathered around sports such as pedestrianism and prize fighting worried the middle classes who wanted to see working men take part in healthy and moral activities. Temperance societies, debating groups, reading rooms, choirs and Christian fellowships were established and encouraged in order to improve the lives and behaviour of the masses. Despite opposition from some Nonconformists, sport too had its place in rational recreation. Following the example of England, the encouragement of cricket by schoolmasters and clergy was driven by paternal concerns for the well-being of children and the working class. Taibach CC was set up in 1843 by Capt Robert Lindsay for men from the local copperworks and colliery. A local newspaper remarked that the establishment of the club 'had a most beneficial effect upon the habits and morals of the young men, withdrawing many of them from the neighbouring taprooms and other places of disreputable resort'.[56]

Football too began to be encouraged within Welsh grammar and public schools and it was in these years that something recognizable as rugby first appeared in Wales. Here the influence of the English public schools was crucial. In the middle years of the nineteenth century, the traditional unruly ball games of the masses were being harnessed in public schools to help control boys and teach them basic Christian values. In fact, these games continued to be very rough but the rules were written up and developed in order to control some of the chaos of the games and allow schools to compete against each other. What really drove the development of public school (and university) football in the middle of the century was muscular Christianity and the associated cult of athleticism. This was an ideology that linked the strong athlete with a religious and political conviction of one's superior social position. Athleticism was thought to help develop character and manliness in the way in which God had intended: the athlete was tough, strong and fair, a leader but able to respect the rules and others. Football was thus thought to be key in the creation of men who would take forward the British Empire and its military might.[57] Despite their reputation for radicalism and even pacifism, the majority of the Welsh people, and particularly the Welsh gentry, were deeply committed to British imperialism.

Thanks partly to masters educated in England, public and grammar schools in Wales, such as those in Llandovery, Brecon, Cowbridge and Monmouth, began to play versions of football in the 1850s and 1860s. As in England, the early games were somewhat haphazard with rules that were yet to be clearly divided between handling and dribbling codes. A student of Christ College, Brecon in the 1860s recalled: 'Our football was somewhat feeble, the game played being a kind of soccer, but with no very stringent rules with regards to hands or offside.'[58] In games between Newport and Abergavenny in 1867 and 1868, players could catch and run with the ball but points were scored by kicking the ball between the posts and under the bar.[59] By the 1870s a handling game appears to have been adopted by the majority of leading south-Wales schools. This move was in common with the minor English schools that tended to follow the influence and example of Rugby School. Thus by playing rugby the Welsh public schools also had an avenue through which to compete and prove their worth against their English peers.

The exact process by which football spread across Wales (and Britain) remains unclear. What is clear however is that old boys of Welsh schools were key to the process. The Neath club was formed in 1871 by a group of solicitors and other professional men, which included an old Llandoverian. In 1861 six students from Christ College, Brecon placed an advert in the local press stating that they would like a friendly game of football with any six gentlemen from the area.[60] A club was formed in westerly Cardigan in 1876 by old boys of the local grammar school. One of the rules of the Cardigan club read: 'Players will please use boots with as few nails as possible, and no iron plates must be worn on the toes of boots'.[61] This tempering of the brutality that marked the game in public schools probably helped the diffusion of football and rugby. Cardiff (formed 1876) and Swansea (formed 1873) rugby clubs both essentially grew out of cricket clubs where players wanted to extend their summer activities. In Newport the early successes of the 'somewhat exclusive circle' of the Newport club (formed in 1875) led to 'an outburst of enthusiasm' for rugby in the town. The club was attracting 400 spectators to its matches by the end of its first season and began charging them 6 *d* entry in its second season. A host of new local clubs were quickly formed, and in recognition of these developments, the club broadened the social base of selection in the 1880–81 season 'to make the team as far as possible representative of the playing talent in the town'.[62] Newport also provides an important clue as to why rugby took off rather than soccer. The club had originally intended to play under the association rules but found it difficult to obtain local fixtures. Once one code of football established something of a foothold in an area, then it made sense for interested players to follow that lead. The speed with which the working classes turned to the game suggests that football was not a completely alien concept to them and that the continuing informal games discussed earlier had survived on a relatively wide basis. The onward march of rugby can be charted by the fixture list. In Cardiff's first season (1876–77) it played just three fixtures, against Newport, Swansea and Merthyr. By 1889–90 the club was playing 35 games a season, including games in the north and south of England.[63]

Early rugby was a very different affair to the later game. Players would just take off their coats and play in ordinary clothes. In some of Cardiff's early games some players did not even remove their bowler hats, while one brave man played in evening dress.[64] Play was based around kicking and prolonged mauls or scrimmages, as they were then known. Passing was not a feature of the game and nor was a clearly delineated playing area. In 1877, at a match between Newport and Rockleaze at Clifton Downs, one player chased a rolling ball for 300 yards before managing to touch it down for a try.[65] One player remembered of the 1870s 'the game was crude and rules were not so stringent, and we had no "words of thunder" from the W.R.F.U. to remind us that football was a game of skill rather than skull cracking . . . the niceties of the game had not been grasped, and there were more barked shins than goals'.[66] An excursionist to Narberth versus Haverfordwest in 1879 was rather shocked: 'The Narberth team seemed ignorant of the commonest rules, and played more like savages than men; the 'scrimmages' seemed more like a free fight than anything else, and in a less remote place the game would have been stopped by the umpire on more than one occasion'.[67] Yet despite such crudity the 1870s marked the beginning of a new era. Even the press was beginning to take notice and regularly report matches thus raising the general profile of rugby. Following the lead of soccer, whose FA Cup was founded in 1871, the South Wales Cup was established in 1877 with Newport beating Swansea in the first final. Although it would be nearly twenty years before the game enjoyed a genuinely mass following, the modern game of rugby had arrived.

V

The industrialization that drove social, cultural and economic change in Wales also created a nostalgia for the rural popular culture of the start of the century. By the end of nineteenth century, urbanization (which itself was driven forward by industrialization) had come to embody spiritual and physical decay, while rusticity was seen as an integral component of Englishness. There were similar sentiments in Wales where urbanization and industrialization were held responsible for the decline of the Welsh language and its associated 'folk' culture.[68] The nostalgia this created for the past meant that *gwylmabsantau*, once attacked as immoral, were now celebrated 'as a symbol of the values of a departed village community whose harmonious relationships had been destroyed by social changes'.[69] Similarly, folk football offered a notable contrast to the growing interest in rugby. *Cnapan* players, after all, were said to play 'not for any wager or valuable thing but strive to the death for glory and fame which they esteem dearer than any worldly wealth'.[70] One journal reader replied to letters enquiring about *cnapan* with:

> If only as a slight protest against the barbarous game as it played at present, I should be glad to see the matter discussed in your columns . . . Hundreds *then* played, *now* hundreds, nay thousands, look on at others playing. There were many thousands present at Shrewsbury on Easter Monday, and the concomitants of betting, drinking, and bad language were fearful to contemplate, while the shouting and horse-play on the highway were a terror to peaceful residents passing homewards.[71]

Time had put a safe distance between him and the mêlées that had offended state and religion at the start of the century. Others also had cause to look back at pre-industrial Wales as a safer age. The minutes of the Taff Ely Rod Fishing Association show that the organization was constantly concerned with the pollution caused to its waters by industrial activity upstream.[72] The impact of industrialization on sport was far reaching.

The nineteenth century may have witnessed significant changes in both sport and popular leisure more generally but there were continuities too. In the 1880s there were still foot races on public highways for wagers but there were also organized athletic meets in specially constructed grounds such as Newport's Rodney Parade. Here, in the late 1870s and early 1880s, professional and amateur runners competed alongside each other, while the crowds were boosted by the peripheral entertainments such as fireworks, donkey races, penny farthing races, brass bands and side shows and stalls.[73] Apart from the entry fees charged, this was not a world away from the wakes of the start of the century or the sports days put on by brewers in the middle of the century. Some aspects of sporting culture, such as the large-scale football games or the widespread popularity of animal sports did of course decline; meanwhile other aspects of sporting culture, such as the numbers who played cricket or watched football, increased. But none of this means there was a complete revolution in sport and leisure as some earlier historians have claimed. Nor was it simply a case of change being imposed from above. What was most common was adaptation and compromise. The traditional game of fives moved from the churchyards, where it offended religious sensibilities and broke windows, to the back of pubs and then specially constructed courts erected by entrepreneurial publicans next to their licensed premises.[74] In the course of this process of adaptation, the game became known as handball. Rugby drew upon the unorganized survival of small games of football but adopted rational rules to displace its unruly history. As we shall see in the following chapter, there were some within the established middle classes who welcomed and promoted this development in the name of civic pride, but there were others who disapproved.

The case for continuity and adaptation is cemented by the nature of social and industrial change. The growth of industrial towns was driven by the migration of people from rural areas. When people moved east and south into the industrial districts they took their culture with them. When William Evans was caught playing quoits in a field owned by the Dowlais Iron Company, he was charged with causing 'wilful damage' (to the extent of one penny) to the company's land. In his defence, Evans explained that 'he came from Cardiganshire, where they were allowed to play where they liked, and having only been in Dowlais for a week, he did not know that he was doing any harm'.[75] The five shilling fine may have meant he did not play again on private land but individuals like him meant that pubs let thirsty punters play in their gardens and fields instead. This movement of people helped ensure that, unlike Irish, the Welsh language was not destroyed by the loss of people to foreign parts. Instead, the migration helped unite and forge a sense of nationhood in what had always been a divided and disparate nation. In the years to come, sport would play its part in giving this sense of patriotism a popular voice.

Modern Sport in an Industrial Society, 1880–1918

On 19 February 1881, a team of Welsh ex-public schoolboys, three of whom would go on to become Anglican clergymen, visited London to play the first ever Welsh rugby international match. The game was not well organized and the Welsh team turned up two players short. One of those who failed to show had been told of his selection after a club game but had never heard anything else or received any official instructions. Replacements were found from Welshmen in the three-deep crowd and the Welsh team members eventually changed into their red jerseys at an inn near the ground. It was, according to an English newspaper, a 'ridiculously easy victory', with England scoring six tries and Wales failing to register a single point.[1] Nonetheless, the match was a portent of the new organized, codified and commercialized sporting culture that was being forged across Wales and Britain at an irregular but hurtling pace.

I

The beginning of international rugby in Wales coincided with an industrial watershed that inflicted huge economic, environmental and social change on Wales. The last quarter of the nineteenth century saw the growth of the export-driven coal industry reach breakneck speed and, by 1911, nearly one in three occupied men in Wales was a miner. The burgeoning coalfields brought massive migration into industrial south Wales. A mass proletariat was created as workers from rural Wales, England, Scotland, Ireland and beyond arrived in search of work and a new life. By the 1911 census, 49 per cent of the population of the Glamorgan coalfield had been born in England,[2] and there were over a million more people in Wales than there had been forty years earlier. The rise of modern sport and an industrial society were inter-related. Within the industrial communities, housing and health problems were rife, but a vibrant culture was forged from within through Nonconformity, music, pubs and working men's institutes, Liberal politics, trade unionism and, of course, sport. This popular, religious and political culture crossed class boundaries and helped to keep a 'frontier society' together and entertained. One player noted, 'The life of the toiling thousands is hard and uninteresting enough, the mind of the professional and business man is vexed with the cares of his occupation, and it is good that football should come once a week to take them out of themselves'.[3] But sport was not just about escape from the dreariness and pressures of daily life: it offered players and spectators physical and emotional expression, a sense of belonging and companionship, a touch of danger sometimes, and a quest for perfection and success. It was not an escape from life; it was a part of life.

A significant proportion of the in-migrants into industrial Wales came from England's West Country, a region where rugby was already established as the dominant local sport. They brought to south Wales an appreciation of the oval ball thus helping rugby, rather than soccer, establish itself as the sport of the region. As we saw in chapter one, this process was aided by the support of the Welsh middle classes who took the sport from their schools to the wider population. Paternal industrialists were also happy to patronize rugby for the working classes. They saw it as a way of keeping their workforces happy and distracted from less morally uplifting pursuits and possibly political activities too. Above all, it was perhaps the sport's ability to promote community loyalty and identity in the burgeoning urban areas that won it middle-class support. At the beginning of the nineteenth century, only one in five people lived in towns. The massive urbanization that accompanied industrialization meant that only one in five lived in rural areas by the outbreak of the First World War. Rugby offered a useful way of binding the new urban communities that were made up of an agglomeration of people from different classes, localities and nations. The Newport club, for example, was proud of having 'no class distinctions' and put its success on the playing field down to this and 'the encouragement of the idea that the Newport XV was a town institution, a symbol of civic unity . . . [and] that the best football talent of the town should be available to win reputation for the town through the team that proudly bore its name and wore the Black and Amber'.[4]

The South Wales Cup (set up in 1877) and the accompanying press coverage provided the burgeoning towns with a vehicle through which they could express their developing civic pride. The competition quickly proved popular with spectators and it encouraged the development and expansion of the sport. A Llanelli correspondent noted of the local club's success in the competition, 'It means raising her name and her fame amongst the towns. It tends to bring more trade, a more vigorous public spirit, and a healthier social life'.[5] Although it drew on and helped feed civic pride, the South Wales Cup was also the cause of disputes, especially over foul play and whether teams were adhering to the regulation that required them to only field players who lived within a twelve-mile radius of the club. Talent was a sought after commodity and bending, flaunting or ignoring the rules was far from unknown. But controversy is the stuff of sport and rugby's popularity and the social base of its clubs grew steadily as the nineteenth century drew to a close. By the 1880s, crowds were beginning to number in their thousands and the charging of an admission fee was becoming the norm. This was enabled by the rise in disposable income and the Saturday half-day holiday that the working class increasingly benefited from in the second half of the nineteenth century. Seeing the rise in such pleasures, those who did not enjoy a half-day holiday increasingly felt deprived. In 1887, the 'clerk fraternity' of Milford Haven wrote to the press to complain that, 'with aching hearts [we] have often longed for an exchange of occupation for the afternoon with those who were free to drive to the Haven, to take a row on the river, to engage in a game of cricket or of lawn tennis, or to fill up that part of the day with some other mode of healthful recreation'.[6]

Not all agreed that watching rugby was actually healthy recreation but its popularity grew steadily, as was evident from the erection of the first grandstand at Cardiff Arms Park in

1881. The working classes played in increasing numbers too and informal and formal teams began to be found in streets, churches, villages and industrial works, sometimes with exotic names such as Rhymney's Pig's Bladder Barbarians and Carmarthen's Diamond Skull Crackers. In 1893–4, a thousand people watched Scotland play England but 20,000 turned out to watch Wales play the English. In 1895 the Welsh [Rugby] Football Union (WFU) had twenty-three clubs; by 1900 the figure was fifty. Not untypical was that of Glais in the lower Swansea valley, where a local colliery manager forged a club out of local miners and metalworkers.[7] Indeed, it was rugby that helped such small industrial communities develop their own identities within the broader canvas of similar pits, valleys and peoples.

By the end of the nineteenth century, rugby had gained its first superstar too. Arthur Joseph Gould was born in Newport in 1864. Like so many others, his family circumstances were a product of the industrialization around them. Gould's father had moved from Oxford to Monmouthshire to work in a brass foundry business. English in-migrants were quickly assimilated into Welsh society, and three of his sons played for Wales, while another three played for Newport. Arthur was the outstanding talent of them all. He made his senior Newport debut at sixteen years of age and was never dropped thereafter. His good looks added to the number of his admirers but he was an all-round athlete, the greatest three-quarter of his generation and, by 1896, rugby's highest point scorer ever. As one excited devotee put it, 'Matchless in skill and grace, a great sprinter who was also a football genius, a man who could swerve both ways at top speed, a player unexcelled in judgment, a wonderful drop-kick, a great punt, he has never had his equal as an attacking back'.[8] These were saleable assets and sport was already becoming a commercial activity. Gould had won over £1,000 in foot races by 1890, and his fame was celebrated in the press, in adverts for chocolate, in music halls shows and even on matchboxes. People went to matches to watch Gould alone, and his celebrity and often breathtaking performances helped Welsh rugby make huge advances in terms of both standards and popularity. So too did his club Newport RFC, who trained, practised and developed new tactics, virtues often not present amongst their contemporaries in the openly professional world of English soccer.

Wales may have played its first international ten years after England and Scotland but it was a significant force in the making of the game. Like modern soccer, rugby teams initially played to no set formation, varying the number of full backs and forwards. But in 1886 Wales played four three-quarters against Scotland, a system which was to become the norm across the rugby world. This was an innovation pioneered by Cardiff RFC, which was so successful that most other senior Welsh sides copied the system. The system took some time to establish itself in the tougher rigours of the international game but it came into its own in 1890 when Wales beat England with a display of short, sharp passing in rainy conditions. With Gould as captain, the first Welsh Triple Crown came in 1893. Welsh international play was enhanced by the end of 1890s by the increasing use of working-class forwards from the Rhondda and other industrial districts. This gave Welsh teams the might needed up front to make the most of the pace and skills of the backs.

Welsh rugby may have been an amateur sport, but a mix of snobbery and a fear that working-class players enjoyed unfair advantage through some innate toughness and a refusal to conform to gentlemanly fair play meant that Welsh rugby never quite sat comfortably alongside the gentlemen players and administrators of England, Scotland and Ireland. When Scotland played in Ireland there was champagne at the post-match dinner; when the Welsh visited they had to make do with beer. In 1903, the Irish wanted to put up the admission prices to keep the 'roughs' out, after the Welsh had broken into the ground and smashed things up the previous year. In 1896, such tensions were brought dramatically out into the open by the setting up of a fund to honour Gould. The inspiration was the benefits that had raised over £9,000 for the embodiment of Victorian cricket, W. G. Grace. The WFU itself gave £50 and the £600 raised in total was used to present Gould with the deeds to the house that he rented. Rugby's International Board however declared that the gift was professionalism and clubs and individuals were banned from playing against Gould. After an outcry in Wales, the WFU withdrew from the International

Board and international rugby. The potential loss of profitable fixtures against Welsh teams was not popular in England and its Rugby Union soon overturned the ban in an open vote, worried about dissent amongst its clubs so soon after the 1895 breakaway of northern teams to form rugby league. The Scots, however, refused to play Wales for two years and suggested that the Welsh would be better off joining the new Northern Union (as rugby league was known until 1922) or forming their own professional game.[9]

English rugby had split into the union and league codes because of the refusal of the southern clubs to sanction the payment of players for the time they lost at work in order to play.[10] Northern Union however soon became fully professional and thus presented Welsh talent with a financial temptation to 'go north'. To the annoyance of supporters, mass defections began; in 1896, for example, six Llanelli players joined Rochdale all at once. A Wigan scout seeking players in Penarth ended up being thrown into the sea, while other scouts were forcibly marched out of towns. One supporter complained in 1897 that 'Llanelli in football has been to the Northern Union what Rhayader is to Birmingham in the matter of water supply'.[11] The most famous of those who headed north in the 1890s were the curly-headed James brothers of Swansea. Labourers in the local copper works in the week, on the rugby field they were entertainers: they dodged, dummied, passed and ran, elevating, as historians Smith and Williams noted, 'artisanship to artistry'. Evan and David James first joined Broughton Rovers in 1892, a transfer which preceded the great rugby split but was the subject of a Rugby Football Union inquiry. The brothers were reinstated to the union game in 1896 but they both moved back to Broughton in 1899 for a £200 down payment, £2 a week and additional jobs as ware-housemen.[12] Yet despite such riches, life was not always easy for the players who went north. David's wife grew homesick and they returned to west Wales where he worked in a copper-works until his death. In the north of England itself there was some discontent that the part-time jobs given to Welsh players were often symbolic. Others complained that the Welsh players were paid so well to play that they did not bother to take an extra job. Players such as the James brothers thus found themselves on the receiving end of some 'brute' and rough play. The cause of the 'Taffies' up north was probably not helped by some of their compatriots taking a signing on fee but then staying in Wales. Others did go north but masqueraded under 'fictitious names', claiming to be 'Welsh players of renown'.[13]

Whether players actually went or were who they claimed to be, the financial rewards available in the north for players who wanted to be paid acted as a safety valve and ensured that the issue of professionalism was not forced back home. The Welsh game was also kept in the amateur fold of the union code by a casual attitude to what amateurism actually meant. By the mid-1880s, clubs were compensating working-class players for the time they lost at work in order to play. However, suspicions that Welsh clubs gave excessively generous expenses, or even basic payments, were constant in and outside the Principality. Yet fixtures with Welsh teams were popular and the English authorities were reluctant to inquire too deeply into the 'shamateurism' of the Welsh game. The WFU made the occasional inquiry and even expulsion but seems to have mostly turned a blind eye to the 'rampant' professionalism in its own backyard.[14] By doing so it ensured that Welsh rugby could remain in the international game and thus provide an outlet for local and national patriotism through regular victories against teams from across the border. This attitude was rooted in the character of Welsh national identity in the late nineteenth and early twentieth centuries. Popular Welsh patriotism was more concerned with achieving recognition within a British context than with separation. Sport offered a perfect vehicle for this: an opportunity to get one over the English neighbour without any of the uncertainties or extremities of a political movement.

There was one brief moment when tensions over professionalism briefly threatened the position of rugby union in Wales. In 1907, allegations of professionalism and match fixing were rife in rugby, not least thanks to accusations and admissions emanating from Aberdare. Out of this crisis came the introduction of professional rugby to the region. In 1907–9, encouraged by promises of financial assistance from the game's governing body, six Northern Union clubs were set up in south Wales by individuals who either no longer wanted to be involved in the dishonest 'shamateurism' of Welsh rugby union or had been suspended by the WFU for having such transgressions uncovered. Due to poor gates and the expense of travelling to the north of England for games, none of the new clubs actually lasted more than five seasons but the episode demonstrated what could happen to the union game if it made too much of an issue out of being strictly amateur.[15] As it turned out, soccer was the real beneficiary of the episode. Some of the Northern Union clubs, such as Mid Rhondda, switched to soccer and the confidence the dribbling code was gaining represented a notable contrast to the recriminations and negative publicity in rugby union. As soccer grew steadily, there were warnings that it was threatening the very existence of rugby in the Rhondda and other localities.[16]

The lure of riches, domestic or northern, was not the only problem rugby had to face. Play could be rough, tough and sometimes violent. Referees were particularly vulnerable to the anger of players and spectators. Such disorder upset not only the administrators, who at times even resorted to distributing copies of the rules amongst the spectators to avert crowd trouble, but also the establishment at large, which already feared the political implications of the social changes that industrialization was bringing. Nonconformity also feared the growing popularity of sport, not just because of how spectators and players behaved, but because it tempted them away from the chapel pews. The Revd John Rees of the Rhondda declared that football was 'the dullest and most senseless game the world had ever seen. Even an ape . . . would not disgrace itself by seeking its pleasures in kicking a football. If their young and middle-aged men wished to frequent pubs, theatres and football fields then let them, in the name of the living God, remain outside the Christian pale'.[17] The close links between alcohol and rugby also upset the Nonconformists. Clubs, small and large, used pubs and hotels to change in, while many spectators drank before, during and after matches. The antipathy towards rugby reached a height during the 1904–5 religious revival, when bible readings, prayer meetings and chapels in south Wales thronged under the zealous influence of the young evangelist Evan Roberts. Drunks forsook the bottle, baritones gave up singing and rugby players burnt their jerseys. One rugby player leapt to his feet during a service and declared: 'I used to play full-back for the Devil, but now I am forward for God'![18]

Yet, for all the importance of the chapel in Welsh life, its influence was not as far-reaching as is often thought. In 1905, within months of the revival blowing itself out, Welsh rugby enjoyed perhaps its greatest moment. In front of 47,000 people, New Zealand took on Wales at the Arms Park at the end of a successful tour that had seen the tourists defeat England, Ireland and Scotland. Wales triumphed by three points to nil, after New Zealand were controversially disallowed a try. Wales had succeeded where the other home nations had failed, beaten the world's greatest team and upheld the honour of the British motherland. The game proved to be a defining moment in Welsh cultural history and cemented the popular relationship between rugby and Welsh national identity that has endured until today. Contemporary Welsh writers got rather carried away and saw the match as a moment of glory for not only a triumphant nation but a triumphant race too. The editorial of the *South Wales Daily News* excitedly declared:

> The men – these heroes of many victories that represented Wales embodied the best manhood of the race . . . We all know the racial qualities that made Wales supreme on Saturday . . . It is admitted she is the most poetic of nations. It is amazing that in the greatest of all popular pastimes she should be equally distinguished . . . the great quality of defence and attack in the Welsh race is to be traced to the training of the early period when powerful enemies drove them to their mountain fortresses. There was developed, then, those traits of character that find fruition today. 'Gallant little Wales' has produced sons of strong determination, invincible stamina, resolute, mentally keen, physically sound.[19]

A nation's progress and the racial superiority of the Celt: the reaction to the victory was indicative of the national confidence and consciousness that abounded amidst the economic and cultural buoyancy of late Victorian and Edwardian Wales. The WFU, established in 1881, was just one of a host of national institutions produced by this vibrant cultural nationalism. The patriotism generated by the defeat of the New Zealanders was further fed as Wales confirmed itself as the leading rugby nation in the United Kingdom. Seven championships and six triple crowns between 1900 and 1911 were a testament to a prowess at rugby and, by extension, of a nation itself. The antipathy towards the game was soon forgotten and rugby, once the victim of Victorian tirades from chapel pulpits, was now a symbol of a proud, successful and respectable nation.[20]

Many of the other symbols of this Welsh nationhood were limited in their appeal but rugby was more embracing and further reaching than Nonconformity, the Welsh language, the Liberal Party or any of the national institutions that it created. Rugby gave a south Wales that was becoming increasingly diverse through the effects of industrialization and migration, an accessible and successful banner under which to unite. Members of the Welsh team that beat New Zealand were actually born in England, yet all were treated as national heroes. Wales was being remade by its people into a popular rather than purist nation. Nonetheless, the ancient game of *cnapan* offered supposed Welsh roots for the sport of the English public schools.[21] As with *eisteddfodau* (competitive festivals of music and poetry), Wales was inventing, or at least rediscovering, traditions through which its new national identity could be legitimized. Meanwhile, the popular base of the sport in south Wales contrasted firmly with the game's middle-class status in England. This further enabled Welsh rugby to be portrayed as something different and unique and a symbol of the cross-class harmony that the middle classes liked to believe characterized Wales. Along with Nonconformity and singing, rugby thus became part of the popular face of a new Wales that was exerting its identity within Britain as an equal but distinct nation. Rugby's adoption into the mainstream of Welsh culture can be traced by the attitude of the greatest Welshman of the era, David Lloyd George. In 1895, he wrote to his wife that the industrial valleys of Monmouthshire were less responsive to his radical politics because their inhabitants were 'sunk into a morbid footballism'. In 1908, he saw his first match when he kicked off Cardiff against Blackheath at the Arms Park. He exclaimed 'It's a most extraordinary game . . . and I must say I think it's more exciting than politics'.[22] Whether he meant it or not, that he said so publicly suggested that rugby was now firmly entrenched in the cultural landscape of Wales.

Welsh success on the pitch was based upon a recognition of the importance of back play that was not to be found in the forward dominated spheres of English and Scottish rugby. Gould argued that the 'world of rugby football has never seen anything to equal the swiftness and accuracy of Welsh passing'. Perhaps more controversially, he claimed that Wales was achieving its results 'with *comparatively ordinary material*'.[23] There was nothing ordinary about the playing skills of backs such as Teddy Morgan, W. J. Trew and Dickie Owen. Furthermore, Wales could also boast probably the greatest player of the Edwardian era, Gwyn Nicholls of Cardiff. Born in the Forest of Dean, Nicholls's international career ran from 1896 to 1906, during which time he won twenty-four caps and captained Wales ten times. Passing was the strong point of his game but he was also a brilliant runner and tackler. After retiring, he continued to exert influence on the Welsh game as a selector for the international XV. A testament to his stature came in 1949 when the Gwyn Nicholls memorial gates were erected at the Arms Park.[24] The popularity of such rugby heroes was illustrated during the 1910 Tonypandy riots. An angry crowd of striking miners smashed and looted shop windows but carefully avoided the chemist shop of Willie Llewellyn who had played on the right wing for Wales.[25]

The Tonypandy riots were one sign that, for all the wider evidence of economic and cultural prosperity, the drive for profit in the coalfields had its victims. Industrial disputes and riots swept south Wales in 1910–12, illustrating that no combination of beer, patriotism and hymns was going to make the working class accept the *status quo* if they felt that their interests were being neglected. The new Welsh national identity was flawed, too reliant on symbolism and unrepresentative of the material interests and concerns of the people of Wales. The dominant Liberal Party was campaigning on issues such as temperance, disestablishment of the Anglican Church in Wales, land reform and the establishment of national educational establishments. To an industrial working class, living in cramped and unhealthy conditions and working in dangerous conditions for wage levels constantly under threat, such issues were hardly a priority. It was thus no surprise that trade unionism was on the increase and the Labour Party was establishing a political base.

The limitations and gradual fragmentation of the Liberal, middle-class vision of Wales were also evident in sport. In north Wales, it was not rugby but association football that enjoyed the support of the workers, thanks at least partly to connections with Shropshire. In 1876, the Football Association of Wales (FAW) was founded by a Wrexham solicitor in response to a challenge for an international match from Scotland, which had already been playing such games with England for four years. Wales lost the match 4–0 and it would be another three years before it scored an international goal. The first Welsh international team was largely made up of professional middle-class men but it also featured a miner, a stonemason and a chimney-top maker. As in rugby, there were no fixed rules to national qualification and the team included a Scottish doctor who had settled in Ruabon and a Shrewsbury solicitor.[26] North-east Wales became the cornerstone of soccer in the Principality and in these early years Wales's international players were mostly drawn from the cluster of clubs around Wrexham and the English border, with Druids of Ruabon, Wrexham and Oswestry being particularly well represented. The Welsh Cup was first competed for in 1877–8, making it the third oldest soccer competition in the world. Wrexham won the competition that first season, although it was another year before the FAW had the money to have the trophy actually made.[27]

As the game developed in north-east Wales over the rest of the nineteenth century, English professional clubs quickly signed up the best players from the region. The greatest footballer of Edwardian Britain, and one of the most influential Welsh sportsmen ever, was Billy Meredith, a former miner from Chirk who played for Manchester City and Manchester United. His career spanned from 1894 until 1924 and featured 1,568 matches and 470 goals. He won forty-eight caps for Wales and would have had more had his English club always released him when he was selected. Crowds flocked to watch Meredith play. He was the original wizard of dribble but he also had a powerful shot that reputedly once broke a crossbar. In 1907, he led Wales to its first ever home championship. Meredith went on playing professionally until he was forty-nine years old and appeared in a FA Cup semi-final in his final season. A controversial character, in 1904 he was fortunate not to be banned for life when he attempted to bribe an opposing player into throwing a crucial league match. He put the year-long suspension he did receive down to anti-Welsh sentiment. No doubt driven by this sense of injustice and his experience of mining disputes, he was a leading light in the fledgling players' union. Like A. J. Gould, Meredith was also a sporting celebrity and a symbol of how quickly sport became commercialized. He advertised goods, had his own sports shop and brand of boots and appeared on stage and in films. Yet Meredith never made his fortune and was repeatedly the victim of bad luck in business.[28]

In both Manchester and his native north Wales, Meredith was accorded idol status but in south Wales he was a famous name rather than a popular hero. The national Welsh soccer eleven was dominated by players from the north and thus it had no popular following in the south. Despite its rhetoric and pretensions, Wales was very much a divided nation. North Wales may have come under Liberal political dominance but culturally, economically and, increasingly, linguistically, it was a long way removed from the coalfields and ports of the south. Rugby however did not enjoy unrivalled access to the loyalties of the sporting public in south Wales at the turn of the twentieth century. Association football in south Wales may not have been able to claim the pivotal role in working-class culture that it did in England and Scotland but the game still enjoyed some popularity in the region. Leagues and small part-time professional clubs existed and from this footing the game's popularity grew. Edwardian in-migration brought men to south Wales from north Wales, the Midlands and other football-following parts of Britain. They brought with them a devotion to the sport, founded new clubs and supported the existing teams. Professional clubs such as Cardiff City (1910) and Swansea Town (1912) were formed which began to compete in English competitions and attract crowds comparable with rugby. Soccer's popularity may have been increasing in the south but it had yet to offer the kind of significant success against outside teams that would reflect well on Wales and give the game an opportunity to become a symbol of national pride. Furthermore, the rise of soccer in the south attracted hostility in rugby circles. There were accusations that it was the game of the alien, driven by professionalism rather than more pure or Welsh ideals. Most of such attacks were not actually under-pinned by hostility towards professionalism or incomers. After all, the renaissance of Wales was based upon the labour of inmigrants and driven by the financial interests of industry. Some of Wales's greatest rugby players were also English-born and hidden payments to such men meant that the sport was hardly averse to paying its stars. Instead, the bulk of the on-slaughts soccer faced before 1914 represented the fears of the rugby fraternity that their sport was being pushed into the background. Such concerns for the future were added to by the foul and defensive play that was seeping into club rugby. The sporting culture of Wales was in flux and rugby, a symbol of national pride, was under threat.[29]

II

In 1889, *The Times* noted it was 'an age for devising new games, borrowing foreign, and furbishing up old ones'.[30] Wales played its part in this age of sporting revolution and innov-ation and was home to a whole host of sports, large and small. In 1895, Rhyl hosted the world's first ever international hockey match, when Ireland beat Wales 3–0. Yet pioneering new sports was no easy task and it required imagination and perseverance. Hockey was predominantly an English public school game and Rhyl possessed the only competitive hockey club in Wales for seven years. Although there were touring matches against English sides, the Rhyl club often had to make do with internal games, such as tall-versus-short, married-versus-single or under-thirties-versus-over-thirties. The club held exhibition matches between its players in neighbouring towns in order to encourage the formation of new clubs. This encouraged new players but had little effect in the formation of new teams. Thus, in organizing the first international, the Rhyl club had looked as far as Oxford University for Welsh-born players and some of the Welsh side had never met before the match. The sport gradually caught on in the south, thanks not least to the work of Newport Athletic Club where it provided an alternative for ageing rugby players, but its growth was not unproblematic and it was 'frequently spoilt by the absolute incompetence' of referees.[31]

In some of the less popular sports Wales was not only one of the earliest international playing nations but it also produced some of the all-time great players. Wales played its first water polo international in 1897, eleven years after the birth of Paulo Radmilovic in Cardiff to a Greek father and an Irish mother. He competed in five Olympic games, the last in 1928 when he was in his forties. Radmilovic won four golds, three at water polo and one in the freestyle 4 x 200 metre relay, and Steve Redgrave remains the only Briton to have won more Olympic golds. He also won the Welsh swimming championship fifteen times between 1901 and 1922 and was still swimming a quarter of a mile a day aged 78. But it was water polo that was his forte where he 'used his speed to the best advantage, whilst his shooting is deadly'.[32] The development of swimming and water polo owed much to an 1878 amendment to the 1846 Baths and Washhouses Act, which enabled and encouraged local councils to build covered swimming pools.[33] The act was not just designed to help the working classes stay clean and healthy; it was also a recognition that local authorities should bear some responsibility for the provision of facilities for physical recreation and sport. A Welsh Amateur Swimming Association was formed in 1897, while south Wales was one of the earliest venues for water polo, especially for women. In 1899, the Swansea Ladies water polo club was founded and it was soon competing nationally. In 1900 the club beat Jersey Ladies to win the Ravensbourne Shield, and it did not lose again until 1907.[34]

Water polo may have had a touch of the exotic about it but other sports were more down to earth. Quoits was a traditional game that involved throwing iron or rope rings at spikes. Like so many other sports, it was updated, organized and codified in the late Victorian period. Wales played its first quoits international in a defeat against England at Cheltenham in 1896. Quoits was a cheap and easy game to play and was especially popular in mining districts. It required less space than football but was certainly as competitive and it drew crowds of spectators to the fields where it took place. Publicans were often involved in organizing matches, presumably in the hope of boosting business. Money was important enough in the sport to cause international contests to be suspended between 1903 and 1911, after a disagreement between the Welsh and English bodies over the sharing of gate receipts and guarantees. The star of Welsh quoiting was William Dice Davies of Aberdare, the 'Grand Old Man of Quoits'. He represented Wales twenty-five times, seventeen of which were victories, and won the Welsh championship five times. Yet quoiting failed to build upon its popularity and never entered mainstream popular culture. It was literally a dirty game, with throwing a heavy ring into a bed of clay often splashing spectators and players alike.[35] Ultimately it was less appealing and less exciting than soccer or rugby. As these sports developed in schools, many children and teenagers were lost to quoiting before they were old and strong enough to throw the heavy rings with any success.[36]

Quoiting may have been playable in any open space but other sports required more specialized arenas and the sporting revolution made a significant impact on the landscape of urban Wales. As well as football and rugby grounds, tennis courts, golf courses and croquet lawns could all be found in the more prosperous centres, particularly the spa and seaside towns, such as Llandrindod Wells or Pwllheli, where such facilities were used to attract genteel visitors and tourists. Sports such as croquet and tennis were distinctly middle class and their appeal rested as much upon their social status as it did on the pleasures of playing. Despite the common public rhetoric that Wales was a democratic nation, the landed gentry and middle classes were often keen to keep their recreation exclusive. This was clear at the Royal Welsh Yacht Club in Caernarfon. Anyone who wanted to join had to be voted in by the members, with just one opposing vote in five being cause enough to fail. This select and sociable club did not want discord amongst its members, and politics and religion were banned from discussion at club meetings. The strict code of conduct was developed with formal dress codes that demanded jackets of slightly different shades of blue for different occasions. As at so many other boating clubs, vessels that were used for trade or charter were banned from the club: this was a retreat for those who could afford to sail simply for racing and pleasure.[37] In a similar exclusive vein, the North Cardiganshire Archery and Croquet Club held expensive balls and insisted on red and cream striped petticoats and white hats for its women members. Not only did such events and requirements add a fun and sociable side to the club's activities, their cost also helped to ensure a certain class of member. Breaking into these established elite circles could be difficult, even for people of financial means and status. A medical family from London who moved to Cardigan Priory offended local standards and manners by proposing themselves as members of the local tennis club. So 'many people threatened to black ball them, that they were warned to withdraw their names'.[38] Golf, almost a middle-class craze by the Edwardian era, was another sport that allowed people to flaunt social status. One letter writer to the *North Wales Chronicle* complained that there were clubs in north Wales where 'it is avowed openly and un- ashamedly that no tradesman need seek to become a member'. This was, according to the writer, 'the unspeakable snobbery of the gentry and professional classes'.[39] Golf's popularity amongst these classes was also enhanced by the fact that it offered a leisurely opportunity to escape the urban environment and could be played all-year round by those whose physical peak had passed and even by women. Whether they played or not, the presence of females in golfing, tennis, croquet and boating clubs meant that sport also had the important social function of providing opportunities for respectable young adults to find romance.

Thus the popularity of such middle-class sporting clubs was rooted in the opportunities they offered for socialising, and no golf or yachting club was complete without its bar. Nonetheless, there were still wider social norms to comply or compete with. Golf was the subject of some distaste in the chapels because people were playing and drinking on the Sabbath. In 1913, three prominent Newport citizens were actually prosecuted for play- ing golf on a Sunday.[40] The Anglican church appears to have been more supportive of such social sports than the Non- conformist chapels. In 1885, Penlleiniau, Pwllheli, got its first tennis club thanks to the encouragement of the local vicar and curate.[41] At the Penarth Yacht Club, there were frequent complaints of bad language, while women were only allowed on the balcony when accompanied by a gentleman. A move to introduce Sunday drinking to the club was heavily outvoted in 1894 by, according to one press commentator, 'frail and haggard men of whom nothing was known but their cheques'. The club minute book noted the proposal was thought to be 'unnecessary, unexpedient and dangerous'. The club members did however have their bar, concert parties, ladies' nights and billiard tables to keep them entertained for the rest of the week.[42] There were, of course, club members who took such middle-class sports very seriously. Tennis, for example, despite its reputation as a flirtatious sport, had a competitive angle and in 1886 Roath and Penarth Tennis Club hosted the first Welsh Lawn Tennis Championships. By the Edwardian period the championship was based at Newport Athletic Club and attracted leading players from across the world.

At the other end of the social spectrum from exclusive clubs where membership was dependent on status were the athletic grounds where all were welcome providing they could afford the entry fee. Such stadiums were found across industrial Wales and were built by entrepreneurs and publicans seeking to cash in on people's desires to watch and bet on races. To draw in the punters, athletic races were often part of bigger galas or fairs, and alongside the professional athletes there were often serious and comic amateur races, brass bands, boxing booths and cycle races to be enjoyed. In 1896, the racing of bicycles on roads had been made illegal and it was this that encouraged the building of crude tracks around the athletic grounds in what was another commercial venture. Cycling already enjoyed widespread popularity in the 1890s as a healthy recreation, although, at first, the sight of women astride their bikes shocked onlookers and raised fears about the implications for female health, while the speed of many youngsters terrified and intimidated other road users.[43] As a sport, cycling had first taken off in France in the 1880s, following the invention of a chain-driven bicycle with inflatable tyres and wheels of equal size. But it also found a popular home in south Wales, and, in particular, in the Cynon Valley where it was the source of immense local pride. Jimmy Michael of Aberaman won the 100 km world crown in 1895, the first British cyclist to win a world title. The Welsh contribution to cycle racing was recognized in 1896 when Newport hosted the world championships. Cycling, like boxing, was a sport whereby artificial stimulants played an important role in boosting performances.[44] Arthur Linton, another world record holder from Aberaman, died of typhoid fever in 1896, aged just 28, but there was speculation that his death was hastened by his use of stimulants such as cocaine. Linton's trainer, Choppy Warburton, was later banned from English tracks, possibly because of doping offences.

For the Victorians cycling embodied modernity but other sports were distinctly more primitive and, as such, existed on the margins of urban life, pushed there by a respectable distaste for their brutality. The continued existence of cock-fighting into the twentieth century, hidden in the backyards of pubs and farms because of its illegality, was one sign that pre-industrial habits died hard. It was not just violence towards animals for which there was respectable distaste. On 'bloody spots' on mountainsides,[45] bareknuckle fighting drew crowds to watch brutal clashes between tough local heroes. Typical was the 1885 contest between two hauliers from Maerdy, who fought in the early hours for £5-a-side on Merthyr Mountain. They had spent the evening drinking, accompanied by a band of 'admirers' who later followed them up to the mountain to enjoy the contest. The fight lasted for an hour-and-a-quarter and left the victor with his eye 'blackened, his lips cut, chin swollen, and hands extraordinarily increased in bulk'. His victim was knocked unconscious. Such bloody fights may have shocked and appalled the press, and the individuals who some-times tipped off the police, but they were popular with the punters who gathered in their hundreds and eagerly betted and cheered on the fighters. Sport was rooted in the wider culture that cradled it and violence was a part of working-class culture. Although often fuelled by alcohol, it was a legitimate way to resolve disputes, personal and even political, and prizefights appear to have been as often the result of individual arguments as they were professional contests. The fights had their own internal rules, which were bound up with notions of 'manliness' and 'honour'.[46] When the police did raid fights and arrest the pugilists, it was a collision of two cultures that judged prize-fighting as either a 'brutal practice' or a 'noble art'.

Boxing never won the support of the respectable middle classes but the introduction of gloved fights in the 1890s at least gave the sport some legal status. The sport's focus then shifted from mountainsides to fairground booths and the halls of industrial Wales. Here, promoted by local entrepreneurs, men fought for fame and purses, large and small. The popularity of these bouts meant that amateur boxing never established the same strong tradition in Wales that it did in England.[47] The booths offered brave punters an opportunity to box against fighters of all standards and such work was an important source of extra income for even the biggest champions. The leading pugilists were as popular amongst the industrial working class as any football or rugby player. Edwardian Wales produced three of the period's greatest boxers. Peerless Jim Driscoll was a flyweight of Welsh-Irish Catholic descent who was brought up in Cardiff's docks. Although he never actually won a world title, he was stylish, courageous and patriotic and one of the era's most famous fighters. Like his contemporaries, he fought benefit bouts for local charities and striking miners, thus ensuring he remained rooted in the community from which he came. In 1925, tens of thousands followed his funeral cortege through the streets of Cardiff. Freddie Welsh, the son of a middle-class Pontypridd auctioneer, ran away to north America but deliberately cultivated his image there by adopting a flashy lifestyle and patriotic surname. He returned to Britain in search of boxing success with sombreros, long black coats and the sense of a showman. At first, his kidney punching and American ways failed to win much appreciation in his native Wales but in July 1914, to patriotic acclaim, he became the first Welshman to win an official world title. He then went back to seek his fortune in the States and after war broke out declared himself an American citizen.[48]

Jimmy Wilde of Tylorstown began his working life in the pits but, despite the disapproval of his chapel-going wife, found it easier to earn money in the boxing booths. He was a hard and fast puncher and became British champion in the early months of the First World War, to the accompaniment of a barrage of middle-class disapproval at men fighting for sport and money when others were fighting for their country. Wilde had refused to enlist and appealed against his conscription. He eventually became a sergeant instructor but continued to fight and won the world flyweight title in 1916. Like Welsh and Driscoll, boxing success made him a celebrity. He made guest appearances in music hall shows and comedy fights in England and even starred in his own film, *From Pit-Boy to World's Champion*. Such public activities stepped beyond the realms of sport and took stars into the wider arena of celebrity and popular culture. Other sportsmen took this step into the glittering world of music halls further. Fred Dyer toured Britain as 'the renowned Welsh singing boxer . . . the most refined and only act of its kind'.[49] The fact that Dyer was Welsh seems to have been important in signalling to prospective audiences his skill as both a boxer and a singer.

Combinations of bad luck, big generosity, foolish investments and the interwar depression meant that neither Wilde, Welsh nor Driscoll held onto the fortunes that their fists and fame won. They died penniless and unremoved from the insecurities of the society that spawned them. Yet in many senses they were the lucky ones. For every champion there were countless others who retired from the ring punch-drunk and penniless. Historian Dai Smith has argued that boxers were emblems of their societies, whether they were the unknowns who briefly sprung to fame before catapulting back down again, their careers metaphors for a society within which uncertain and sometimes fatal futures were commonplace, or the world champions whose triumphs represented the hopes of a people and whose physical but directed skills embodied the attributes workers valued.[50]

III

For those who sought to escape the harsh industrial world that boxing encapsulated there were more rural sports. Snowdonia became one of Britain's leading centres for mountaineering, a sport that combined an aesthetic appreciation of the natural world with the thrill of challenging its dangers. Yet for the Welsh, the mountains were a place for work rather than play and the majority of mountaineers came from the English middle classes. The background of such participants not only ensured that mountaineering was out of place in Welsh popular culture but it also created the paradox that while the mountains have Welsh names, their rockfaces, overlooked by locals, often have English names.[51]

Cricket may not have strictly been a rural sport but it had all the image of one. The social base of the game continued to broaden in the north and south as more clubs were formed by pubs, churches and, despite some continuing Nonconformist opposition to sport, chapels. Between 1870 and 1885, 91 teams were formed in Cardiff alone. As in rugby and football, some of these working-class clubs enjoyed patronage from 'above', in the form of help with land and money, but others were a testament to how working-class culture could be self-sufficient. Cricket also grew in the middle-class suburbs where it helped bond the residents of these new and expanding communities. The game may have been growing but there were also worries that Welsh cricket was becoming insular and falling behind English standards. Inspired by developments in rugby, a South Wales Cricket Challenge Cup was launched in 1879, which did much to increase the popularity of the sport. But it also created bad feeling between teams and led some to think that cricket was losing its gentlemanly image. The cup was disbanded in 1886 after many teams pulled out to avoid arguments over fair play and accusations of shamateurism. In 1888, Glamorgan County Cricket Club was formed at the Angel Hotel in Cardiff after the old South Wales club collapsed. It played its first match in 1889 against Warwickshire and entered the Minor Counties competition in 1897, a competition in which it never excelled. The new county was formed to give cricket a higher outlet in the face of domestic uncertainty but it also reflected the burgeoning identity and confidence in Glamorgan itself and united the county's east and west after the tensions of the cup. As Glamorgan CCC sought higher standards, it increasingly turned to English professionals. In 1889, just an eighth of Glamorgan players were born in England; but by 1896 the figure was over half. Despite the use of working-class professionals, the patronage of the middle and upper classes was key to the club. Notably, the wealthy Brain brewing family, who moved to Cardiff from the West Country, did much for the club and sport, on and off the field. The Marquess of Bute meanwhile, whose influence was key in the making of the Cardiff landscape, allowed Cardiff Arms Park to be used by Glamorgan CCC, gave the club financial support and became its first president.[52]

Senior cricket of course extended beyond Glamorgan CCC. Monmouthshire joined the Minor Counties competition in 1901 and it was joined by Carmarthenshire in 1908, although the latter failed to win a game in its first two seasons and pulled out in 1912 after failing to achieve a secure financial base. The one-day game also developed as a series of working-class leagues were created across south Wales in the 1890s. By 1900, there were approximately twenty teams playing cricket in Swansea alone.[53] The best league clubs employed professionals and in 1907 Llanelly CC signed Ernie Vogler, a South African bowler and one of the best players in the world. The excitement of league cricket and the higher standards that accompanied professionalism attracted players and crowds to Welsh cricket. By the outbreak of the First World War, the old country house teams had all but disappeared and cricket was part of a sporting culture that was still socially divided but certainly more populist.

In Aberystwyth in the 1890s mixed cricket matches took place with the men batting with broomsticks or bowling and fielding left handed. Such humorous spectacles typified the way that sport was seen as a tough, physical and manly arena, unsuitable for women who were popularly thought to be delicate, frail and even uncompetitive by nature. The Victorian and Edwardian ladies who did play sport were usually the subject of disgust or ridicule. Male competitors in a rowing race at Penarth Yacht Club simply refused to compete against a lady who dared to enter. Middle-class educational institutions provided one haven where sporting women could escape such censure. Women's hockey was introduced into the University College at Aberystwyth in 1893 but, despite the players' ankle-length dresses, it was another six years before male spectators were allowed to watch their games. Men were attracted to watching women's sport by curiosity as much as by voyeurism. In 1895, Cardiff played host to the British Ladies Football Club before a crowd of 3,000. Standards of respectability however demanded that the goalkeepers, required to dive around after the ball, were men.[54] The gentle and relatively unphysical games of golf, archery and croquet were much safer sports for females and in 1905 the Welsh Ladies [Golf] Union was formed, the first national sporting body for women in Wales. Such sports however were distinctly exclusive and for working-class women there were fewer sporting opportunities than for anyone else in society. Even at school working-class girls found their physical education limited to marching and drill.

IV

For all the pride and patriotism associated with Welsh sport during this era, Wales was also a country that was immensely proud of its Britishness. When Queen Victoria died in 1901 rugby matches in Wales were postponed as a mark of respect. But it was the First World War that most clearly demonstrated that Welsh national consciousness co-existed with a sense of British and imperial pride.[55] The outbreak of war in 1914 was celebrated by cheering crowds in Welsh streets, as the nation joined the rest of Britain in standing as a people united against a foreign aggressor. As men flocked to recruiting offices to volunteer to fight, all rugby matches were suspended to help the nation concentrate on the push for victory. In contrast, but with the support of the War Office, the soccer authorities in England and Wales argued that matches were needed to maintain morale at home. The sight of people watching football while others fought 'the greater game' in France shocked many, and the early weeks of the war saw Welsh and English newspapers print angry and disgusted letters:

> It is unimaginable that people could look on at a game of football and forget themselves in the ecstasy of a winning goal at the moment when their comrades, maybe brothers, are making gallant and stupendous efforts at the front, even sacrificing their lives for the life of the nation.[56]

Sports players themselves were also the target of many calls-to-arms. They were, after all, strong and fit young men. The WFU marvelled, 'If only every man in every first XV in Wales were to enlist, what a magnificent body there would be at the service of our country.'[57] The frenzy of disgust against professional sport gradually died down as it became apparent that many soccer players had enlisted and that crowds were falling thanks to travelling restrictions, longer working hours and fewer evening kick-offs. Such restrictions eventually led to the suspension of professional soccer at the end of the 1914–15 season. For Wales there was one great achievement that season. Swansea Town became the first Welsh team to reach the second round of the FA Cup when it beat the Football League champions, Blackburn Rovers, in front of 16,000 people at the Vetch. Although it lost to Newcastle United in the second round, the club had achieved one of the game's biggest ever upsets. For the men in uniform in the crowd, who were all given half-price admission, it must have been a welcome distraction from the war.

Amateur sport continued rather haphazardly throughout the war. Senior and junior soccer clubs, for example, played friendlies and irregular games in makeshift regional leagues. Sport also played an important part in the life of the armed forces, as it offered some temporary relief from the horrors of the trenches and the tedium of camp life. Boxing was especially popular and its physical contests fitted in with the rhythms and needs of military life. For women at home there were some significant advances in sporting opportunities during the war. Most munitions factories in Britain had women's football teams. Munitions girls had already broken the normal standards of female conduct and propriety by working in factories but, having done so in the cause of patriotism, they were beyond reproach. Thus playing football was just one new social liberty that came their way, alongside a degree of sexual licence and the freedom to use pubs without compromising their social standing. Such freedoms proved short-lived for most women and in 1922 the FAW followed the English FA in banning women from playing football on grounds under its jurisdiction.[58]

The First World War was the first modern industrial war and it was industrialization that underpinned the establishment of a modern sporting culture in late Victorian and Edwardian Wales. It created an industrial proletariat that sought the physical and emotional recreation that could make tolerable a life of manual work. It created a middle class that saw sport as a means of socially bonding its dispersed self, as well as keeping the workers healthy and loyal to wider concepts of community that extended beyond class. Some members of this middle class also saw there was money to be made in sport and publicans in particular were important in developing sporting facilities such as bicycle and athletic tracks. Similarly, the world of the music hall and seaside also developed in this period, as a new commercial mass culture was built to serve the industrial proletariat's desire to spend its rising disposable income in search of pleasure. Industrialization brought massive in-migration to urban Wales, first helping establish rugby as the sport of the masses in south Wales and then bringing soccer to the nation as a whole. Sport also offered migrants a way of keeping in touch with each other and their cultural roots. In the 1880s, a group of Yorkshire men in Cardiff formed White Rose Cricket Club, while Scots there set up Caledonian CC. Irish immigrants in the city played hurling and Gaelic football amongst themselves, while the football teams of the Catholic churches in Merthyr were the subject of both Irish pride and prejudices.[59] The maintenance of such identities was not at the expense of wider integration and sport played its part in helping people belong to their new communities and nation. The historian Linda Colley has argued that 'Identities are not like hats. Human beings can and do put on several at a time.'[60] While sport gave voice to many local identities in many different sports, it also helped give a popular voice to the Welsh patriotism that was forged on the back of the economic buoyancy that industrialization brought. Winning at sport was sweet, but it was all the sweeter when done in the noble name of one's nation. Such celebratory patriotism was not dissimilar to the cause that sent thousands of young men to their death in the trenches of the First World War.

3

War and Peace, 1918–1958

Eight-and-a-half million people lost their lives in the First World War; nearly 40,000 of them were Welsh. Amongst this number was a host of sportsmen, famous and not so famous, including eleven Welsh rugby caps. Welsh football's most famous casualty was the maverick Sunderland goalkeeper Leigh Rhoose who was killed in the battle of the Somme at the age of thirty-eight. Such losses cast a long shadow over sport in the 1920s, just as they did over the rest of society. WFU officials and players visited the London Cenotaph on the morning of each Welsh international at Twickenham. Welsh fans, players and officials paid similar respects before Cardiff City's FA cup finals of 1925 and 1927. Individuals learnt to cope with what they had witnessed or lost in their own ways. For some, no doubt, sport helped them recover some form of normality but for everyone the memories were never far away.

I

Many men who had served in the armed forces returned with a new or stronger passion for organized sport. Sports had been actively encouraged by the army and played in every training camp and even at the front, helping make the lives of troops more bearable. Many rugby enthusiasts from south Wales who had joined up probably found themselves playing soccer for the first time. Fed no doubt by this broadened appreciation of the dribbling code, professional soccer built on its Edwardian foundations and belatedly matured in south Wales during the short-lived post-war economic boom.[1] By 1921, Cardiff City, Swansea Town, Newport County, Merthyr Town, Aberdare

Athletic and Wrexham were all in the English Football League. Smaller professional clubs were set up in nearly every significant town in south Wales, by professional and small businessmen looking to boost local civic pride and their own personal prestige. This all raised the popularity, profile and standard of the game in Wales immensely. Success quickly followed, most notably at Cardiff City. The 1920s were a great decade for the club, as it rose from the old Southern League to the Football League's first division and attracted crowds of up to 50,000 to Ninian Park. In 1924, the club missed out on the first-division title by 0.024 of a goal (rather than goal difference, a system of goals scored divided by goals conceded was used to separate teams then). Had it not missed a penalty in its final game then Cardiff City would have won the title. That season, the club had seventeen internationals on its books, including the captains of Wales and Scotland. During the 1920s, City enjoyed the best FA Cup record of any club in England and Wales. It was beaten in the semi-final in 1921 and then 1–0 by Sheffield United in the 1925 final, courtesy of a defensive error. In 1927, Cardiff reached the cup final again, but this time defeated Arsenal 1–0 after Len Davies, Arsenal's goalkeeper who hailed from the Rhondda, let a seemingly weak shot slip through his hands. An estimated 40,000 people travelled up to London that day from all over Wales. The team was not just representing Cardiff but the whole nation. As the newspapers of the day remarked, this was not just Cardiff City against Arsenal, it was Wales against England. Over-excited reporters on both sides of the border spoke of Celtic invasions and Welsh warriors coming to take the English cup away. Fans wore leeks (so many people bought them that Covent Garden tripled the price of the vegetable for the day), carried flags bearing the Red Dragon, sang 'Land of my Fathers' and made sure that London knew the Welsh were in town. In the morning, many people spent their time sightseeing and drinking but not everyone went to the match. Some wives and girlfriends made the most of the trip and went shopping and exploring while their men were at the game. Back home, people gathered around radios in homes, shops and streets to listen to the first ever live broadcast of a FA Cup final. In Cathays Park in Cardiff the council put up loudspeakers and a crowd of up to 10,000 listened closely to the match.

The news of the victory was received amidst scenes reminiscent of 1905, as Cardiff and the whole of Wales united in jubilation. When the victorious team returned to Cardiff two days later, an estimated 100,000 people turned out to welcome the heroes home. For those on the streets that day, and for the rest of Wales, it was a rare moment of triumph during a period of severe economic dislocation. In subsequent weeks the team was given civic receptions in other Welsh towns, north and south, while the trophy itself was displayed in a local department store for all to see. Despite the fact that only three of the team were actually Welsh, the game was portrayed by the press as a national achievement. The players' identities as individuals did not matter; collectively they were playing for Wales and had won the English cup. There was the odd dissenting voice of a bitter rugby enthusiast or a cultural purist who objected to the idea that an assorted team of professionals from the four corners of the United Kingdom could bring glory to Wales, but such killjoys were very much in a minority. And besides, the team had been captained by Fred Keenor, an uncompromising and rugged defender who was Cardiff-born-and-bred.[2] The lack of success elsewhere in Welsh public life was enough to overcome most residual doubts about professionalism or the idea of soccer as an English sport. The huge crowds that Cardiff City attracted in the early 1920s were no more attached to the club's Welsh players than they were to its English ones. It was the talents and abilities of individuals they admired, not nationalities; working-class culture was essentially meritocratic.

The Welsh Rugby Union (as the WFU became known in the 1920s) tried to react positively to the threat of soccer, staging schoolboy internationals in smaller towns such as Pontypridd and Aberdare, and giving grants to junior leagues and struggling clubs.[3] Llanelly RFC, the dominant Welsh club of the 1920s with its entertaining and high-scoring play, also offered some hope that the Welsh game could withstand the rise of soccer. The club stood firm against not only the formation of a professional soccer club in its town but against what it perceived as the reluctance of the WRU to pick its players. It certainly boasted some fine players, most notably Albert Jenkins, a pacy centre who scored points with aplomb and could kick the ball the length of the field with either foot. Llanelli idolized him, helping him to resist £500 offers to go north, but the WRU only gave him fourteen caps. At a time when the international and domestic game was largely bereft of outstanding back players, such ignoring of talent did not help the national team and the 1920s was an inauspicious decade for Welsh international rugby. In 1930, even the Lions chose Howard Poole, the Cardiff scrum half who was yet to be capped by Wales. Although Wales won the championship in 1922, the national XV won only nine out of thirty-two games between 1923 and 1930 and failed to beat England once in this period. In 1928, even France beat Wales for the first time. The team lacked stability as well as flair. In 1924, thirty-five different players and four different captains were used. That year Wales lost to Scotland 35–10, its heaviest defeat since 1881. Welsh fortunes were not helped by a number of men born in Wales playing successfully for England. When England convincingly beat Wales 18–3 in 1921, the victors had five men from the Principality in their line-up. In an amateur sport with no clear rules on nationality and that operated within an economically mobile wider society, it was not surprising that such ironies occurred. They were no different from the English-born players who had donned the red jersey before the First World War when economic pulls operated in the reverse direction.

It was not just to the English union game that Wales was losing talent. In the inter-war years, Welsh rugby union haemorrhaged talent to northern rugby league, to the great expense of the national side. Around 900 Welshmen, including seventy internationals, joined rugby league between 1919 and 1939.[4] At the 1939 Rugby League cup final between Salford and Halifax half the players were Welsh. The gut reaction of the WRU to such losses was to lash out. In 1927, a rugby league match was held on the welfare ground that Ebbw Vale RFC played on but neither owned nor controlled. The WRU threatened the club with expulsion.[5] Perhaps one of Welsh rugby's biggest losses was Jim Sullivan. Aged just seventeen, he joined Wigan from Cardiff in 1921. He proved to be a full back of immense talent and one of the greatest ever players of rugby league. A masterful attacker, defender and leader, his greatest forte was his powerful kicking which earned him 2,867 career goals. He won sixty league caps for Wales and Great Britain and his twenty-two goals in a single match remains a Wigan record. Sullivan, an apprentice boilermaker, went north because he saw 'little prospect of securing another job' in the economic climate of the 1920s.[6]

The economic condition of Wales was at the core of the exodus north. When the guns fell silent in 1918, industrial Wales moved quickly through a short economic boom into the depths of the depression. New trading patterns, overseas producers and technologies emerged, robbing the south-Wales coal industry of many of its markets. The long-term short-comings in its production methods were exposed and its prosperity collapsed. Being so reliant on one industry, the result for south Wales was mass unemployment. In 1920, there were 265,000 miners employed in south Wales; by 1933 the figure was 138,000. Faced with falling wages and lengthening dole queues, the mining unions fought back but, after the disaster of the General Strike and the subsequent lockout, their power was crippled. After a number of brief revivals, the terminal nature of the change was confirmed by the shock-waves that followed the Wall Street crash. The coal industry was brought to its knees and the early 1930s saw unemployment reach cataclysmic levels: 43 percent in the Rhondda, 59 per cent in Merthyr and 76 per cent in Pontypridd. Although pockets of relative stability existed, particularly in the western anthracite coalfields and the more economically diverse coastal towns, the mass in-migration of the Edwardian years went into reverse, as over 400,000 Welshmen and women left for the greener economic pastures of the Midlands, the south of England and beyond.[7]

The loss of players to rugby league was thus part of a wider movement of people. In such an economic climate, the offer of a signing-on fee plus regular wages was too much to resist for many men, in or out of work. A pedestrian international could attract a lump sum of £250 and £3 for a win, £2 for a draw and £1 15s for a defeat, plus a local job courtesy of his new club chairman. The average weekly wage of a Welsh collier in 1930 was £2 3s 9d. Jim Sullivan received a signing-on fee of £750. The losses to rugby league were unsurprisingly heaviest in Eastern Glamorgan and Monmouthshire where un-employment was the highest. Yet moving north offered no guarantees of an easy life or even better wages. Uncapped Dai Davies felt he was better off at Neath RFC, where he was un-officially getting £3 a week plus the wages from his job, than he was when he turned professional with Broughton Rangers where he had no extra work. What drove him north was a desire to escape the mines but settling down was not easy. He had never left Wales before and his English was poor.[8]

It was not just through the poaching of players that rugby league threatened the Welsh game. In 1921, internationals between England and teams of Welshmen 'gone north' began, and in 1935 France was added to the regular fixtures. The majority of games were held outside Wales but Pontypridd, Llanelli and Cardiff all hosted matches. Attendances were relatively healthy and peaked in 1935 when 25,000 people saw Wales crush France at Stebonheath Park, Llanelli. The speed and handling of such games presented a welcome break from the dour kicking of Welsh rugby union. Yet defensive Welsh press coverage still tended to make unfavourable comparisons with the union game, while spectators were often rather unsure of the rules. Nonetheless, Wales won the rugby league European championship three consecutive times between 1936 and 1938. Despite the spectacle and speed of the international contests, the league game never really caught on in Wales itself. In 1926, after the closure of the local semi-professional soccer team, a professional rugby league club was formed in Pontypridd but it struggled on and off the pitch, winning only eight of its forty-two games. The club withdrew from the league after less than two seasons. Pontypridd also became home to some small amateur rugby league teams at this time but, with the WRU banning even amateur league players from returning to the union code, the future for Welsh rugby league remained in men going north.[9]

II

The depression brought social and cultural devastation to industrial Wales. Many of those still in work were on short-time or reduced wages. To make ends meet, even rugby inter-nationals could find themselves turning out for Wales in the afternoon and then heading back underground for the night shift. Those out of work often did not have enough money for food, let alone entertainment. Attendances collapsed and rugby and soccer clubs resorted to begging and borrowing from the local community and the sporting authorities. For clubs of all sizes such efforts were often in vain and small rugby and soccer teams collapsed *en masse*. By 1928, Ebbw Vale AFC and Barry Town were the only Welsh clubs left in a Southern League that had boasted a Welsh section in the early 1920s. Aberdare Athletic and Merthyr Town slipped out of the Football League and towards bankruptcy, unable at first to employ quality professionals and soon unable to employ anyone. Even in the relative prosperity of Wales's largest city, Cardiff City FC and Cardiff RFC struggled in the face of much reduced gates. Two years after winning the FA Cup, the ageing Cardiff City team was relegated from the first division. Falling attendances meant the kind of quality and expensive signings that the club had made in the early 1920s were now impossible. By 1931, it was in the third division with gates sometimes as low as 2,000. It was the loss of the club's traditional support from the mining valleys that hit Cardiff City the hardest. In the valleys themselves even well established clubs such as Treherbert and Tredegar RFCs folded. Nor was international rugby safe. The WRU's takings halved during the 1920s, and just 15,000 people watched Wales play France at Swansea in 1927. It was not just working-class spectator sports that were affected by the depression. In 1932, the ladies' section of Ystrad Mynach golf club complained that the club was losing revenue because members were leaving the district.[10] In 1935, Ffestiniog golf club closed owing to the lack of transport to the course and the wider economic problems. Yet the club largely consisted of teachers, bankers, clergy and gentry. In the hope of securing a financial future, club management hoped that local quarrymen would take up the sport.[11]

The inter-war years were not a period of uniform economic and social misery for Wales. Llanelly AFC and RFC both enjoyed some success and financial stability in the 1930s, thanks to the relatively more prosperous economic conditions in the tinplate and anthracite coal industries of west Wales. In 1928, seven players in the Welsh XV played for Llanelly RFC. The vibrant popular culture of industrial Wales was battered by the depression but it did not collapse. Musical and religious pursuits continued, albeit on a smaller scale, offering some relief to the suffering communities. Meanwhile, a new communal protest, against company unionism, the ravages of the dole queue and the means test, emerged, providing a glimmer of hope and self-respect. Although money prevented some of the out-of-work from joining sports clubs, sport did play its part in keeping up the spirits and self-esteem of the unemployed. Billiards, snooker, darts and table tennis were popular with the unemployed in clubs and pubs, where they also enjoyed 'fierce conversation' about boxers and footballers.[12] Soccer and rugby teams and leagues for the out-of-work were set up by those concerned about how the unemployed used their enforced leisure time. Sacrifices on food or other 'luxuries' could be made to save money for a big game, while fans could resort to forceful tactics, such as charging the gates, sneaking in or demanding a reduced entry, to ensure they did not miss out. And there were always newspapers to make sure people could read the results and enthusiastically debate the merits of sportsmen, national or local, whether they had seen the game or not.

Betting on sport was especially important in giving the unemployed and wider working class some hope, fun and the opportunity of winning enough money for 'a few comforts'. Indeed, in 1928, police in Cymmer noted that despite the considerable poverty in the area, betting was actually on the increase.[13] Gambling was an integral part of working-class culture, and the wider way in which people enjoyed sport. Horses, greyhounds, fights, pigeons, foot races, football of both codes: if it was competitive people could and would bet on it. Since the 1906 Street Betting Act, gambling with cash had been illegal. Bookmakers would usually only give credit to those who could easily afford to pay and the act was designed to prevent the workers frittering their money away on idle bets. (The credit flutters of their betters, who could afford it and supposedly knew when to stop, was not seen as a matter for the law.) Thus much of the betting taking place on sport was actually illegal. Throughout the inter-war years, the press regularly reported that unemployed miners across south Wales had been prosecuted for running illegal gambling schemes. Yet the bookie, complete with his look-out who watched for any policeman who might come round the corner, was a common sight on the streets of urban Wales and Britain. Indeed, he was popularly thought of as offering a social service. The most popular way to bet on sport was the football pools, whereby punters would fill in a coupon predicting draws and then pay their stake after the games had been played, thus side-stepping the law. Some punters had scientific methods for their predictions; others relied on random numbers and did not even like football. By the 1930s, between five and seven million people in Britain were playing the pools, and as many as one in five of them were women. It was the dream of a big win and the pleasure of the uncertainty that drew people to the pools, but the reality of most people's experience of gambling was a little fun and maybe a small profit.

Working-class athletics was a long way removed from the amateur world of Olympism; it was a sport dominated by gambling and money. The writer George Ewart Evans, who grew up in Abercynon in the 1920s, ran and coached professionally to help fund his university ambitions. The most prominent athletic meet in Wales was Pontypridd's Welsh Powderhall, with its £80 first prize for the 130-yard sprint. It attracted local men, runners from all over Britain and even touring athletes from Australia. Yet, despite the prize monies on offer, even the best athletes could be hampered by their material circumstances. Les Thomas, a railway worker, finished second in the 1929 Welsh Powderhall in borrowed pumps that were a size too big and stuffed with newspaper in the toes. Bookmakers and athletes rigged some races 'to get in a few extra quid'. Indeed, the bribes could be bigger than the prizes and since bookies often paid for athletes' training and accommodation expenses, there was perhaps a degree of obligation to repay the patronage.[14] It was probably common knowledge that many athletes did not always run to their potential, either to raise their odds for subsequent races or to ensure the victory of an outsider. Nonetheless, enough races must have been 'real' to ensure that the watching and betting public did not lose interest.

Another sport that struggled to stand in the economic blizzard was cricket. Glamorgan CCC had been elevated to the first-class counties competition in 1921. The club won its first senior match, against Sussex at the Arms Parks, but then, giving a taste of what was to come, slumped to eight successive defeats and finished the season bottom of the championship. For the rest of the decade, the club struggled with debts, a paucity of young talent and a financial inability to attract good professionals. To try to broaden the club's support, games were held beyond Cardiff, Swansea and Glamorgan itself. Pontypridd, Cowbridge, Neath, Llanelli and Newport all hosted occasional first-class county fixtures during the inter-war years. Although county matches began when most fans were at work, cricket's increasing popularity as a spectator sport was indicated by the 25,000 crowd that turned out to watch the second day of Glamorgan versus Australia at St Helen's, Swansea in 1926. The popularity of county cricket was helped by the continued development of the league and club game across north and south Wales. The 1920s saw the formation of a number of regional leagues, notably the South Wales and Monmouthshire Cricket Association, which was set up in 1926. By the early 1930s, crowds of 2,000 to 4,000 people were common in its first division and it became increasingly dominated by teams from industrial works.[15] Teams might not have always used whites or grass wickets but the game did enjoy a widespread popularity amongst the working class. In the valleys, where space were severely limited, miners often played on levelled coal tips with special rules governing where the ball could be hit. For children and the more casual games there was waste colliery timber for bats and zinc sheeting for wickets. Improvization meant that a lack of resources need not hold back sporting participation.

Glamorgan CCC's fortunes did improve in the 1930s, not least thanks to Maurice Turnbull. Turnbull, a former public schoolboy from a Penarth ship-owning family, made his Glamorgan debut in 1924, aged eighteen. He was appointed captain in 1930 and club secretary in 1932, scored almost 18,000 runs and gained nine caps for England. He was the first Glamorgan player to gain this honour but his collection of caps could have risen had he not fallen out with the MCC over his rule breaking while he was Glamorgan captain. Turnbull also played for Cardiff RFC and won two rugby Welsh caps and three Welsh hockey caps. His organizational skills were key in rescuing Glamorgan CCC from near bankruptcy and to its taking over of Monmouthshire in 1935. Turnbull attended Cambridge University and shared many of the class snobberies that characterized first-class cricket. He insisted that professional players travelled separately from the amateurs and made an appointment if they wanted to see him. On the pitch, Glamorgan's fortunes were helped in the 1930s by the emergence of Emrys Davies as a genuinely talented all rounder. He begun his career with a Llanelli steelworks team and made his county debut in 1924. Davies went on to take 885 wickets for the county, to score over 26,000 runs and to win a single English cap in 1928. He retired from playing in 1954 after a thirty-year career in first-class cricket.[16]

Another of the key personalities in the history of Glamorgan CCC was Wilfred Wooller. He was born to English parents in Colwyn Bay and excelled at both cricket and rugby whilst at school in north Wales. His senior cricketing career began with Denbighshire in the minor counties league and then continued with Cambridge University. He made his Glamorgan debut in 1938 and quickly became a leading light in the county side. Wooller's involvement with Glamorgan was thanks to his friendship with Maurice Turnbull, with whom he played rugby for Cardiff RFC. In 1933, whilst still at school, Wooller made his rugby debut for Wales in an impressive match that saw Wales secure its first ever win at Twickenham. He was the first north Wales schools player to win senior honours and went on to win eighteen caps.[17]

Wooller was one of a number of talented young players emerging in Welsh rugby during the 1930s. Another was Haydn Tanner, an industrial chemist who played for Swansea and Cardiff and is regarded as one of the all-time great scrum halves. Although the club game often remained dour and drab, results improved at international level and the crowds began to grow gradually thanks to a slow recovery in the south-Wales economy and something of a revival in the Welsh tradition of exciting backplay. In 1936, the international against Ireland at the Arms Park was witnessed by an estimated 70,000 people (the ground's official capacity was 56,000). The overcrowding was exacerbated by people breaking into the ground and inside a man was killed in the crush. In the chaos outside, the fire brigade had allegedly turned a hose on the crowd in order to control it.[18] It was something of a miracle that such accidents were not more common at the most popular inter-war football and rugby matches. Although a new £20,000 double-decker stand was built at Cardiff Arms Park in 1934, grounds were crude with rudimentary facilities. Huge crowds could pack on to unterraced earthen or ash banks, where they were in danger from overcrowding, pushing and swaying. Yet, for those who stood there, the banks and terraces were places of affection from where they cheered and cursed their teams.

On these banks was a sea of cloth caps and working-class faces, while in the more expensive stands the supporters were predominantly middle class. Watching sport was an over-whelmingly male-dominated activity, although the small sprinkling of female faces in the crowd was slightly more concentrated in the comfort of the stands. This socially mixed but divided male audience was a constant feature of rugby and soccer before 1939. The composition and character of the Welsh XV itself was changing during the 1930s, as an increasing number of educated players, students and professionals dominated the sport's elite for the first time since the late nineteenth century. Traditional sources of Welsh talent were drying up, as economic problems forced large numbers of working men to reduce their sporting activities or leave Wales altogether in search of work. Policemen, a stable and secure occupation in a time of mass unemployment, became the backbone of many rugby teams. Between 1923 and 1939, there was an average of ten policemen in Cardiff's first XV every year.[19] These policemen were not always popular. Their role in industrial disputes meant they were seen as being on the wrong side of the community divide, while their occasionally violent tactics in controlling striking men could be a source of deeply felt resentment. Clashes on the pitch offered both sides an opportunity to settle such scores. A policeman who badly beat a striking miner from Cwmtwrch was crippled for life the next time he played rugby against a Swansea Valley team. The trouble was serious enough for the police to encourage soccer rather than rugby, while one referee in Glyncorrwg took to the field with a revolver.[20]

In 1935, following the lead of Swansea RFC three months earlier, Wales beat New Zealand to jubilation across the

A regional sport: Newport Baseball Club, 1912. Photograph © National Library of Wales.

Learning to play within social norms: Aberaeron school girls' hockey team, 1904.
Photograph © National Library of Wales.

Welsh working-class icons: Jim Driscoll on his knees against Freddie Welsh, 1910. Photograph © National Library of Wales.

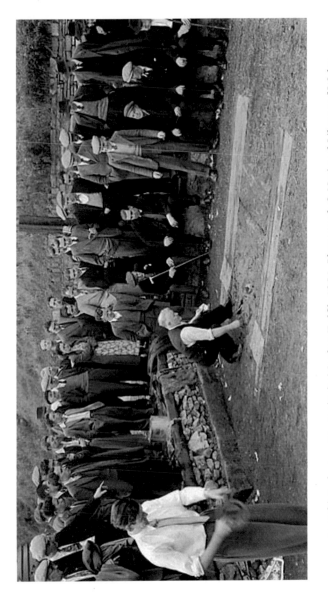

A working-glass game: quoits in Merthyr Tydfil, 1951. Photograph © National Library of Wales.

A genteel sport for both the sexes: Victorian croquet. Photograph © National Library of Wales.

Mixing pleasure with displaying social status: golf in Radyr, Cardiff, early 20th century. Photograph © National Library of Wales.

A cultural landmark in the history of Wales: the Welsh team that beat New Zealand in 1905. Photograph © Welsh Rugby Union Archives.

*The other national game: Cardiff City's Fred Keenor with the
FA Cup in 1927. Photograph © Richard Shepherd.*

The lure of sport: a packed Wembley for Cardiff City's FA Cup win.
Photograph © Richard Shepherd.

The greatest Welsh sportsman ever? Gareth Edwards.
Photograph © Western Mail and Echo Ltd.

Welshmen and a Welsh club in that most English of games: Allan Watkins and Wilfred Wooller of Glamorgan County Cricket Club. Photograph © National Library of Wales.

Black, Welsh and world class: Colin Jackson.
Photograph © DPA DEUTSCHE PRESS-AGENTUR/DPA/EMPICS.

Overcoming sport's prejudices towards women and disability:
Tanni Grey-Thompson, one of Wales's most successful athletes ever.
Photograph © Gareth Copley/EMPICS

Sport's multiple identities: Ryan Giggs, a Welsh Mancunian.
Photograph © Western Mail and Echo Ltd.

Beating the old enemy and reviving former glories: Wales defeat England during the 2005 Grand Slam. Photograph © Photolibrary Wales.

The passions and patriotisms of sport.
Photograph © Photolibrary Wales.

Principality. The social diversity of a team that included colliery workers and Oxbridge students reassured those fearful of rising left-wing sentiments in a depressed industrial Wales. The *Western Mail* thought it 'a victory that is probably impossible in any other sphere'.[21] Such evidence of social unity in an era of increasing class tensions helped cement international rugby's place in the fabric of Welsh public life. The 1920s development of a tradition of hymn singing at matches furthered the sport's association with the passionate but orderly and respectable working class that the middle classes liked to believe in. A writer from England noted that 'Rugby football in South Wales produces an almost religious enthusiasm, and the Welshman has a wonderful power of giving vent to his religion in song. Certainly I have never witnessed anything comparable in emotional excitement to the scene before an international match at Cardiff'. The singing of *Hen Wlad fy Nhadau* particularly stirred him: 'That famous song is full of such pent-up fervour that it is hard to bear with any attempt at outward decorum. It is not so much a challenge to the enemy as a universal and tremendous prayer for their overthrow'.[22] Such singing could also be heard at away matches, when thousands of Welshmen headed off to support their boys, see the sights and make the most of a trip that was usually the result of months of saving. In 1934, 15,000 Welsh men and women made the trek north to Murrayfield, many making the journey by twenty-seven special trains. In 1938, with up to 20,000 Welshmen expected to make the journey, a rail company drafted in Welsh-speaking staff 'who will help through microphones and loudspeakers to guide and direct passengers at Princes Street Station and also be at barriers to act as interpreters when necessary'.[23] Such exoduses were not just limited to football and rugby; special trains were put on from south Wales to the Grand National in Liverpool.[24] Sport offered those who could afford it a multitude of opportunities for a day out.

A *Western Mail* rugby correspondent wrote in 1930, 'A Rugby international penetrates and permeates Welsh life to an extent that nothing else is capable of doing . . . Welsh life in all its many facets is never so truly represented at any national event as a Rugby international match in Wales. Creeds, political opinions and social distinctions are all forgotten'.[25] This amounted to little more than wishful thinking. Sport did not stop people thinking or acting politically, and for much of the working-class Welsh patriotism sat quite comfortably alongside a wider consciousness of class. Alongside the Welsh hymns, leeks and other national emblems that characterized big football and rugby matches against English teams in this period were the same music-hall songs, drinking and rowdy behaviour that were prominent in football in England. For all the claims of Liberal Wales to be a place apart, industrial Wales was very much rooted in the wider culture of working-class Britain.

International football in Wales entered a new period of success in the 1930s, with a national eleven dominated by men from the south Wales valleys who were employed by English clubs. Crowds flocked to cheer their victories but the successes were never treated as national achievements in the way that international rugby or club football's greatest moments were. The players concerned, such as Merthyr's Bryn Jones, whose 1938 £14,000 transfer from Wolves to Arsenal made him the UK's most expensive player, were heroes in their hometowns but elsewhere they were as much associated with their English clubs as they were with Wales. They had left Wales along with thousands others in search of employment and were thus symbolic of Wales's economic paralysis. Their achievements with the national team were joyously celebrated but, like Scots playing in England, never with the same intensity or public acclaim as the heroes who stayed at home. Indeed, the success of the team brought a degree of sadness at the state of Welsh club football. The year 1933 saw Wales's first overseas football international, a 1–1 draw with France in Paris, but Welsh football remained decidedly insular and convinced of the superiority of the British game. The FAW obediently followed the English FA's line on international soccer and declined invitations to join FIFA and its new World Cup.[26]

In 1932, Wales became the second of the home nations to cap a black player in football. John Edward Parris, born near Chepstow to West Indian parents, played for Bradford Park Avenue. His selection was not symbolic of any significant racial tolerance in Wales and it proved to be his only cap. Like

Tewfik Abdullah from Egypt who played professionally for Bridgend Town in the early 1920s, he was tolerated as something of an exception. Where it existed in more concentrated numbers, the black population of Wales was often excluded from sport. Cardiff's ethnically mixed docks suffered from 'a complete absence of outdoor facilities such as football and cricket pitches, bowling greens or swimming baths'. Black cricketers and footballers from the district suffered from popular prejudices that meant that white teams were reluctant to play against them. They were thus limited to playing out-of-town matches, usually for charity, where they presented a curious spectacle that was immediately greeted with such cries as 'look at the black men playing cricket'. More sinister was the prejudice of the miners that poured into Cardiff to watch international rugby and soccer and who often finished their trip with a visit to the pubs and prostitutes of Tiger Bay and a fight with the local 'darkies'.[27] Wales, like the rest of Britain, was a white man's country.

III

The inter-war years were a period of commercial and consumer development, as well as economic misery. For those in work, there were new and fun ways to spend one's money and make life more interesting. Many of those who left industrial Wales did so to work in the new factories of the Midlands and south of England that churned out radios, cars and other new consumer goods. By 1935, half of all Welsh households had radio licences.[28] The wireless proved an important invention in both developing sport and making the lives of millions more interesting and entertaining. In 1927, Wales versus Scotland became the first live rugby international to be broadcast from Wales. By 1939, even quoiting internationals were being broadcast. Not only did such broadcasts make sporting events more accessible to the British population at large, they also helped make sport into an important component of a shared national culture.[29] Highlights of the sporting calendar, such as test matches, the Derby and the FA Cup final, which are too often seen as English rather than British institutions, all attracted eager listeners across Wales. While the radio offered people entertainment in the home, the cinema promised glamour, escapism and a night out. It was, in the words of one historian, 'the essential social habit of the age'.[30] Courtesy of the news-reels, it also offered audiences an opportunity to see footage of sports events. Yet, despite the popularity of the wireless and the cinema, it was the local and national newspapers that were the key components of the sporting media. Press reports let people know how their (and others') teams and heroes had played when away and were also a source of news, gossip and forecasts. The Saturday evening football specials in particular were read avidly by fans of both soccer and rugby. Horse racing was another staple of newspaper sports columns but pigeon racing, quoits and other less mainstream sports also enjoyed significant coverage. The leading reporters became influential and famous figures in their own right. Fans turned to them to represent their views, while selectors and directors listened to them. In a pre-television age, they were the essential link between the sports community and its public.

Motor sports were another area of technological development in the inter-war years. Pendine Sands in Carmarthenshire had been used for motor-cycle racing since 1905, often with crowds of several thousands watching professional riders from beyond the English border. During its 1920s peak, crowds at the Welsh TT at Pendine could reach 20,000, although given the min-imum protection they received from the speeding bikes it is a surprise that accidents were no more than occasional. Taking part in motor sport remained somewhat exclusive, although the growth of the motor engineering industry and mechanical experiences gained during the First World Ward did open up the activity to limited numbers of working- and lower middle-class men. Between 1924 and 1928, Pendine was also used as an official venue for successful attempts on the world land-speed record. Such attempts effectively came to an end with the death of J. G. P. Thomas, whose car crashed at 180 mph.[31]

Hoteliers and publicans must have loved the races because it brought them business. Similarly, newspapers covered such events and the associated sporting gossip because it sold copies. For all sport's claims that it promoted wider social and moral values, there was no denying that it was part of a wider commercial leisure industry, even if clubs rarely made much profit. One sport in which there was money to be made, and which thus attracted promoters in search of profit rather than prestige and civic pride, was greyhound racing. The sport grew out of the tradition of hare coursing and whippet racing across rough ground, but the use of electric hares was an American innovation and commercial companies set up electric greyhound tracks across Britain in the mid-1920s. It was, in the words of one Rhondda writer, 'the new industry of Britain's distressed areas'.[32] This helped ease the financial problems of some existing sports and venues, as greyhound companies took over stadiums such as Taff Vale Park in Pontypridd and Newport County's Somerton Park. By the 1940s it was difficult for the Newport County team to schedule training session because of fears that the players would observe the dog trials and pass on tips to the public.[33] In 1927, to the horror of some members of the WRU, greyhound racing began at the Arms Park, which was owned by a private company. Such was the demand for greyhound racing that, in 1928, the Greyhound Racing Association (South Wales) Ltd built the Welsh White City in Cardiff with an estimated capacity of 70,000. Many tracks in the valleys were not electric and featured dogs owned by local miners rather than companies or tracks. It was often joked that the owners of racing dogs 'lavished much more attention on them than they did on their own brood'.[34] In contrast to horse racing, greyhound racing offered working-class punters affordable opportunities on weekday evenings to bet and see their chosen animals in action. The *Western Mail* crowed, 'it is almost impossible to imagine a more exciting or intoxicating spectacle than five or six of these beautiful creatures straining every nerve in their efforts to overtake the elusive hare . . . [It is the] biggest thrill it is possible to experience in the space of thirty seconds'.[35] Another commercial venture was the Chepstow racecourse, opened in 1926 with Jockey Club approval in 400 acres of parkland. Chepstow racecourse remained fairly inaccessible and on the margins of national racing until the opening of the M4 and the Severn Bridge in the 1970s. Indeed, horse racing never attracted the same level of popularity in Wales that it did in England.[36] Nonetheless, in 1933 the racecourse gained fame in racing circles when Gordon

Richards rode all six winners on the first day of the meet and the first five on the second.

Another sport in which there was money to be made was boxing. There was a continuation of the Edwardian circuit of promoting fights in local halls for a profit but Wales's impact on international boxing was less significant than it had been before 1914. One Welsh fighter who did make an impact was the heavyweight Tommy Farr. Born in 1913 in Clydach Vale, Farr was the son of a haulier who had emigrated to south Wales from Cork. His early boxing experience was in the booths and fairgrounds of south Wales, where he fought exhibition matches for small sums and wagers. He went underground at fourteen years of age and later said 'After the mines, what is fighting? Fighting is child's play.'[37] Farr's heyday came in 1937, when he took on the black American fighter Joe Louis in New York for the world title. In his native Rhondda and across Wales, the fight, broadcast live on the wireless, was followed and hyped like any big rugby or soccer match. To industrial Wales, Farr was 'one of us', a former miner who never forgot his roots. He took to the ring wearing a cape emblazoned with the Welsh dragon, put up a valiant fight and lost on points. Afterwards he went on air and told the people back home that he had done his best and shown plenty of guts. Like the society ravaged by unemployment from which he came, he had never given up but had been beaten by a stronger force. Here truly was a man of his people. The fight earned Farr £36,000, a sizeable fortune, and he lived a glamorous life of fine wine and film stars that was far removed from his native Rhondda. Yet, by not forgetting his roots and by losing, Farr remained an essentially Welsh hero.[38]

Other sports may not have been as dangerous as boxing but they were often just as hard. The world of local soccer and rugby reflected the tough and physical nature of life in working-class communities. For every professional match that took place, there were countless more games, far removed from the world of commercial sport, played in parks, on waste ground and in the streets. In both football codes, tackles, bodies and fists were hurled through the mud, cinders and sawdust of the rough pitches that were built on parks, mountainsides and scrubland. For many youths, giving and taking such knocks was part of a wider process of socialization: playing sport was an experience that helped teach them what it meant to be a man. Furthermore, without this personal experience of the game, the thousands who flocked to see the senior games would never have emerged in the numbers that they did. The most important local matches could attract crowds of several thousand that spilt onto the pitches, but other games were highly localized events, watched by just a handful of friends and family. Local sport was intensely competitive: winning was important. The habit of 'pot hunting', whereby teams entered competitions beyond their immediate area in search of glory, typified this attitude. But, win or lose, for many men and boys, playing sport was a source of considerable physical and emotional reward.

Other local sports were less physical but equally as competitive. Darts, dominoes and billiards flourished in pubs and clubs, to the extent that there were fears that education was being marginalized in working-men's welfare institutes.[39] A Welsh darts championship was founded in the 1930s, which supplied entrants for the very popular *News of the World* championship. Pigeon racing was particularly popular amongst the miners, who kept birds in their back yards, harboured secret feeding and training methods and enjoyed small flutters on the outcome of keenly contested races. Pigeons could also be the source of local pride. When a bird belonging to a Rhondda collier beat pigeons from the Sandringham loft, a national paper ran a headline: 'A Welsh miner beats the Queen'.[40] Baseball was another sport on the fringes of popular culture but which was deeply competitive and imbued with notions of local, class and national pride. Welsh baseball was not the American version but a hybrid closer to rounders. Its popularity was limited to Cardiff and Newport, where, in working-class districts, it surpassed cricket as the primary summer sport. Despite its geographical confines, there was a reluctance in the game to adopt the American rules for fear of losing something Welsh, unique and supposedly superior. Its leagues and associations had national titles and its representative matches against Liverpool (the only other part of Britain where this version of baseball enjoyed any popularity) took place as England versus Wales internationals.[41]

The popularity of baseball was limited by problems of space. At a time when even football pitches were in desperately short supply in industrial districts, the possibility of securing access to the larger spaces that baseball required was remote. The provision of public parks had grown slowly but steadily since the end of the Victorian era but sporting facilities within them remained significantly over-stretched and subject to local regulations governing behaviour and access. In 1938, there were fourteen cricket pitches, forty baseball pitches, forty soccer pitches and nine rugby pitches in Cardiff parks. But this had to cater potentially for over 8,000 schoolboys, as well as the thriving adult leagues.[42] The situation in Cardiff had actually improved after Nazi Germany's expansionist ambitions created a new impetus for the provision of playing fields across Britain. Sport's role in creating a fitter nation was acknowledged and efforts were made in the late 1930s to improve the municipal provision of playing fields and other sporting facilities. In industrial districts, miners' welfare schemes and paternal land-owners were key in ensuring that people had somewhere to play. The more progressive companies were also important in providing both facilities and kit. Lovell's, a Newport confectionery company, provided both its male and female employees with football, grass and table tennis, bowls, athletics and cricket. The company's welfare policy was said to be an 'antidote to labour troubles'.[43] Time was another key resource that people required to participate in sport. This led to the setting up of a summer football league in the Vale of Clwyd in 1927. Most of the teams were comprised of farm workers who worked all Saturday and thus played in the light Saturday summer evenings. However, such out-of-season football was never sanctioned by the FAW and thus had to operate beyond the recognition of the wider soccer community.[44] In urban areas, workers employed on Saturdays played on their half days. Wednesday leagues could be found in the larger towns, with teams full of shopworkers and so forth. Although most workers outside service industries gained a Saturday half-day in the late nineteenth century, it still often did not leave miners enough time to wash before heading off to watch or play sport. Thus in the valleys of south Wales, miners with blackened faces were common sights on and around the pitches. Access to other sports continued to be restricted through social snobberies rather than actual material inequalities. This was not to the taste of everyone in the social elite; a member of Penarth Yacht Club remarked in the early 1920s, 'I can never understand why we don't admit local tradespeople into this Club. There are good men amongst them'.[45] One thing that working- and middle-class sports did have in common was the sociability and companionship that they provided. The minutes of middle-class havens such as the St Fagan's Lawn Tennis Club show that the arranging of dances and teas took up as much committee time as sport itself did.[46]

It was at school that most boys first played organized sport. Compulsory state education began in 1870, but it was not until after the Boer War (1899–1902), which created widespread concerns about the health of the working class, that physical education was positively encouraged in schools. Yet, even then, practices varied and much depended on the voluntary efforts and whims of individual teachers. At Hermon elementary school in Pembrokeshire, the headmaster appreciated cricket because it encouraged the children to develop their numerical skills. A Welsh Schools Rugby Union was set up in 1903, when there were already five schools leagues in existence.[47] The Welsh Schools Football Association followed in 1912, with the objective of the 'mental, moral and physical development of schoolboys'.[48] Yet drill and marching still remained the most common form of physical education. In 1919, a Breconshire doctor complained that in Wales, 'the bulk of our children grow up without having been taught to play, and are almost untrained in body. The scrappy experience of "drill" has done little or nothing for them. It was a dull and weary business'.[49] Physical education did gradually expand through the inter-war years but it remained very much dependent on the whims of local teachers and was particularly underdeveloped for girls. After the Great War, an increasing number of grammar and secondary schools turned to rugby because of the game's amateur ideals and soccer's alleged lack of patriotism during the war. Amateur rugby was also deemed to equip boys with physical and moral qualities that would benefit them in later life. Thus support for schoolboy rugby was intended to produce better citizens as well as better players. Soccer, however, continued to hold sway at elementary schools across Wales and, as in rugby, its achievements were celebrated as moments of genuine civic pride. The 20,000 crowd that watched Swansea Schoolboys win the English schools shield at the Vetch in 1939 was nearly double Swansea Town's average gate that season. The pride in school sport represented a notable contrast with the irritation that ball games in the street caused. Whether played by children or youths, such games were often seen as an unruly hazard to passers-by and nearby windows. Battles with the local policemen, who tried to clamp down on such 'disorder', entered children's folklore but many unfortunates still ended up in court for simply playing in the street.[50]

IV

The Second World War proved to be a very different conflict from the First World War. British military casualties were significantly lower but the bombing of cities such as Cardiff and Swansea meant there was a greater danger to civilian lives. Big sporting venues were requisitioned by the military but sport was also used as a way of maintaining morale at home. Charity games, friendlies and services matches saw players guest for teams near their military base and amateurs and professionals play alongside each other. Even Sunday games were allowed, while the league/union distinction was lowered in rugby, with men who had gone north returning to play union again. Some clubs, such as Newbridge RFC, were kept relatively intact because most of their players were miners, a reserved occupation exempt from conscription. This laid the basis for some post-war success for the club. Internationals continued through the war in both rugby and soccer, with some dazzling displays and victories for Wales in the former thanks to the use of league players. As the historians of the WRU remarked, this was a 'bitter-sweet reminder of the talent drained from Wales in the thirties'.[51]

After the war, sport provided a symbol of what people hoped would be a new era of international co-operation when in 1945 Moscow Dynamo toured Britain. The Russians played Cardiff City before a crowd of 31,000 and exchanged flowers for miniature miners' lamps before kick off. City's 10–1 defeat was a sign that continental football was beginning to make advances that would leave the game's British motherland trailing behind. With few other leisure activities available, spectator sport reached new heights of popularity in the years immediately after the war. In 1946–7, Cardiff City's average league gate of 28,604 was the highest in England and Wales outside the top two divisions. The following season, the club's average attendance was 37,871, the second highest outside the first division. Even Wrexham FC enjoyed an average gate of over 11,300 in the 1947–8 season.[52] In Welsh club rugby this peak of popularity was more extended than in soccer. In 1951, a world record for an ordinary club match was set when 48,500 people watched Cardiff play Newport, the two great Welsh club sides of the 1950s. Even in the late 1950s, matches between the two clubs were still drawing over 30,000 people. However, it was in cricket that the first significant Welsh sporting success took place after 1945. Although still mourning the loss of Maurice Turnbull, its captain and secretary who was killed in Normandy in 1944, Glamorgan secured the county championship in 1948 under the captaincy of Wilf Wooller. It was a team of excellent fielders whose stars included Norman Hever, a young quick bowler from Middlesex, and Allan Watkins who won 15 English caps.

There was limited success for Wales's soccer clubs in the early post-war years. Billy McCandless, who had managed Newport County when it won the third-division south championship in 1939, repeated the feat with Cardiff City in 1947 and Swansea Town in 1949. In 1952, Cardiff City was promoted back to the first division. However, the decline in sports attendances after the post-war boom was already becoming apparent and the club's first season back in the top flight saw an average attendance of 23,000. However, an attendance record for Welsh club football was set in 1953 when 57,893 people watched Cardiff play Arsenal. Four years later, Cardiff City was relegated. Despite such local successes, it was increasingly common for football fans in Wales to have both a favourite Welsh and English team. In Welsh streets, children mimicked both English and Welsh heroes from football and cricket, 'whose names we knew from radio commentaries and whose faces were familiar from smudgy photographs in the press'.[53]

Despite the idolatry bestowed upon them, the players in the professional football teams were essentially ordinary working men, rooted in their communities. Ken Hollyman, a mainstay of Cardiff City's 1947 third-division championship side, frequently had a queue of people waiting for autographs outside his small terrace house.[54] Despite football's maximum wage, the best players' earnings did comfortably exceed those of a skilled worker. There were also under-the-counter payments, benefits, bonuses, international fees and even advertising contracts to boost incomes. But the short nature of a football career meant that the best players did not have the financial means to escape their roots. For the journeyman footballer, wages could vary significantly according to luck, injury and the circumstances of his employer. Financially, he might be no better off than his peers in the pit or on the shopfloor, and many regretted the lost opportunity to learn a trade for later life.

John Charles, a Swansea boy who signed for Leeds United as a youngster, broke away from these restrictions when he joined Juventus in 1957 for a record British fee of £65,000. He signed not only to earn more money but also because he felt he would be treated better.[55] Charles was a powerful centre half and centre forward. In a portent of future developments, he employed an agent and enjoyed a luxurious income and lifestyle. Unusually for a British footballer abroad, the 'gentle giant' was a great success in Italy. He scored 93 goals in 155 appearances for Juventus, who won the Italian championship three times in his five years there. Back home, moves like Charles's helped increase pressure for the abolition of the maximum wage, which finally came in 1961. Another Welshman and powerful centre forward, Trevor Ford, also played his part in undermining the maximum wage. He was suspended after he admitted in his autobiography to receiving illegal payments from Sunderland FC. This forced him to move abroad to play in the Netherlands. Charles and Ford were two of a number of talented Welsh footballers who emerged in the 1950s but continued to be snapped up by English teams. Others included Cliff Jones and Terry Medwin, who set the Spurs team alight, and Ivor Allchurch, an inside forward of immense talent for Swansea Town, Cardiff City and Newcastle United. Thanks to players of such quality Wales qualified for the 1958 World Cup finals in Sweden under the management of Matt Busby's Manchester United assistant Jimmy Murphy. The team got off to a slow start with three draws but a play-off victory against Hungary earned Wales a place in the quarter-finals against the eventual winners Brazil. The Welsh team was eliminated by a Pelè goal in a 1–0 defeat, but the campaign remains the peak of the Welsh international team's history.[56]

The end of the Second World War brought first austerity and then prosperity to Britain. Welsh industry was revived practically through the economic boom and symbolically through nationalization. The dark days of the 1930s seemed over and Welsh rugby shared the nation's rejuvenation. Rugby Union's infrastructure and facilities were improved, clubs increasingly became social centres open to women and children, and a new generation of players emerged. In 1950, Wales won its first outright Championship and Triple Crown since 1911, with a team of fit ex-servicemen, manual workers and products of teacher training colleges. Between 1950 and 1956, Wales went on to win the championship three times and share it a further two times. In the 1950s, Ebbw Vale RFC emerged as a new force in club rugby, driven by the expanding local steel industry and the strength of the many forwards that it supplied the club with. In north Wales, however, rugby remained marginal; in 1948 there were just seven clubs in the North Wales Rugby Union that had been formed in 1934–5.

Like the footballers of the 1950s, the players in these rugby teams were men rooted in their communities but, unlike the footballers, they were amateurs. This enabled rugby international Ken Jones to also compete in the 1948 Olympics, where he reached the 100 metres semi-final. The amateur status of rugby also kept alive the threat of rugby league. To help keep this spectre at bay in west Wales, St Helen's continued to be used for internationals until 1954, despite the ground being dated, raising less in gate money than Cardiff and suffering from heavy traffic congestion. The amateur ideals of Welsh rugby were encapsulated in the international fly half Cliff Morgan, who was brought up in a Rhondda Nonconformist home 'where Mam ruled and Sunday was for chapel'. His appeal ran beyond traditional Wales and he took up an influential radio career with the BBC, where he unashamedly celebrated the moral and traditional values of sport.[57] Yet, for all the ideals of Morgan's world, Welsh rugby offered its players more tangible rewards. Even for decent junior players, rugby could act as a form of freemasonry, opening doors to better jobs. There were also more direct payments for playing, such as cash in brown envelopes, generous travel expenses and free beer. Yet there were no norms and some of the prouder clubs refused to get involved in such transgressions, relying instead on their prestige to attract players.

V

The traditional ideals encapsulated by Cliff Morgan were particularly influential in rural Wales. A study of a Merioneth village in the late 1940s noted that 'nobody likes to be thought of as a gambler, and betting on horses or football pools is uncommon'. Success through gambling contravened the local belief in 'getting on' through hard work, unless the gain was by someone who had suffered hardships despite their own efforts.[58] Gambling may have been considered unsavoury but sport was still a part of respectable rural life. The spread of the wireless, and later television, ensured that national events at Cardiff, London and beyond could be followed in the depths of Caernarfonshire or Cardiganshire. Like choral events, sport was also an outlet of local pride and togetherness in small rural communities. In a village in northern Montgomeryshire, the tug-of-war between neighbouring hamlets was the chief event of summer sports days and the subject of 'much local patriotism'. Local youths would practice it, alongside their jumping and running, for a week or two before, coached by older villagers.[59] Even at the end of the twentieth century, the tug-of-war was an important sport in rural Wales, with the hierarchy of agricultural shows providing a competitive structure for local teams that culminated in the Royal Welsh show.

Ronald Frankenberg's study of a football club in a north Wales village argues that it was a 'symbol of village unity and cohesion'. It occupied a central place in village social life because the 'honour of the village and its place in the outside world are at stake in each game and in the day-to-day conduct of the club'. The fund-raising events of the female-dominated supporters' club were important community events, whose beneficiary was in many ways incidental to the social purpose of the coffee mornings and so forth. Nonetheless, rifts based on personality, class, language, gender and local parochialism adversely affected the club's committee and its running took on many of the characteristics of an introspective and tense rural community life. Like many teams in urban Wales, the club was also caught between just wanting a team for local men to play in and seeking out greater success on the pitch by using better players from elsewhere.[60] This tension between the desire for success and the wish to encourage participation is a theme that continues to cause difficulties for sports authorities today.

The range and organization of participatory sports continued to develop in the inter- and post-war years. For example, a Welsh weightlifting foundation was founded in 1927, while in 1930 the All Wales Ladies' Lacrosse Association was established. Women's sport remained underdeveloped throughout the period, although netball, developed for girls in the late nineteenth century as a less physical version of basketball, was gaining in popularity. It was especially popular in Welsh schools and, in 1947, the Welsh Netball Association was founded. Bowling was important in providing sporting opportunities for older men and women. In 1957, the Welsh Bowling Association could boast 260 clubs and over 15,000 active players. In north Wales however it was crown green bowling that held sway.[61] The Welsh Amateur Gymnastic Association was formed in 1902 and proved to be a sport in which Wales enjoyed some success in the years around the Second World War. Arthur Whitford, of the Swansea YMCA, was the leading British men's gymnast from the 1930s until the early 1950s. He won Olympic and World golds and became a British Olympic coach. Half the British gymnastics team at the 1952 Helsinki Olympics were Welsh. At the same Olympics, Lt Col Harry Llewellyn won a show jumping gold on a horse called Foxhunter. It was a reminder of the diversity of Welsh sport and its popularity beyond the cauldron of working-class culture. Freddie Williams of Port Talbot was world speedway champion in 1950 and 1953. Speedway was a product of the increasing commercialization of sport in the inter-war years. In the 1920s, it could be found at the Welsh White City, but in the 1950s Grangetown stadium played home to the Cardiff Dragons and even hosted the 1952 World Speedway Championships. As one fan remembered, 'The roar of the motorbikes, the smell of the fuel and the clouds of shale dust thrown up as the riders rounded a bend all made it very exciting'.[62]

In 1958, Wales hosted the Sixth British Empire and Commonwealth Games, the biggest sporting event ever held in Wales. Thirty-five nations sent 1,122 athletes (962 male and 160 women) to compete in nine sports (athletics, boxing, cycling, fencing, lawn bowls, rowing, swimming and diving, weightlifting and wrestling). Howard Winstone's boxing medal was Wales's only gold, but there were three silver and seven bronze medals. The Arms Park, complete with its red cinder running track assembled on the dog track around the pitch, provided the focal point of the games and a new stand was built for the occasion. The north too shared in the event, with the rowing held at Lake Padarn in Snowdonia. A legacy of the games was the Empire Pool, built in central Cardiff by the city council at a cost of more than £700,000. Although they had only been able to proceed thanks to personal guarantees made by individuals to the tune of £22,000, the games were a financial success, selling 178,000 tickets and making a record profit of £37,000. The games were also the venue for the popular announcement that Prince Charles would be known as the Prince of Wales, a symbol of Wales's long-held Royalist sympathies.[63] But the games also signified future changes in sport. Firstly, South Africa's participation led to strong protests from multiracial Commonwealth nations, a signal of the increasing politicization that sport would undergo. Secondly, television took images of the games and Wales around the globe. The advent of television in the 1950s did not change the basic appeal and excitement of sport but it did expand the numbers that were able to witness it. Furthermore, television led to radical changes in the running and structure of sport, and it ushered in a sporting climate where money talked to an extent that the sports men and women of the first half of the twentieth century could never have imagined.

4

The Television Era, 1958–2000

In 1964, a PE teacher from Bridgend Grammar School unexpectedly secured the long jump gold at the Tokyo Olympics. Lynn 'the leap' Davies was one of 'the last generation of pure amateurs' in athletics.[1] He made very little money from his sporting prowess and resented the financial restrictions placed upon him. In 1972, he was one of a number of top British athletes who signed an open letter of protest to the Amateur Athletic Association over amateur regulations. Yet, despite the limitations placed upon his earnings, he enjoyed respect and fame across the UK thanks to television coverage of his performances and his success on *Superstars*, a television show that pitted sportsmen against each other in events beyond their normal specialism. Lynn Davies was thus an athlete whose career straddled two different sporting ages. In the thirty years after his retirement, the money that television brought to senior sport would transform it beyond recognition, leaving stars such as Davies to wonder at what they could have earned had they been born a generation later.

I

Davies's position, as a world-class athlete who enjoyed few financial rewards for his endeavours, was not dissimilar to that of the stars of Welsh rugby's second golden era. The Welsh teams of the 1970s ensured that Wales and rugby would be umbilically linked in the popular imagination. Yet, from the late 1950s to the mid 1960s, there were few immediate clues to what lay ahead. Not helped by an Arms Park pitch that seemed to be a permanent quagmire, the national side failed to produce any sustained success. In 1962, it scored just nine points in four games and failed to manage a single try all season. Wales did share the championship in 1964 and then won it in 1965 and 1966, but, in 1967–8, the national team won only one of five games and used three captains. The spectre of rugby league also continued to hover over the Welsh game. In 1967, the threat again became reality when David Watkins, the Newport fly half and Welsh captain, joined Salford for a record £16,000. Supporters also seemed to be losing something of their enthusiasm for the union code, with rugby attendances across the UK in decline. The rise of Saturday afternoon televised sport, increased car ownership and higher earnings had all amplified the available alternative leisure pursuits and reduced the appeal of watching local sport in the cold. The increasingly defensive nature of club and international rugby did not help, and the game's authorities set about trying to boost the popularity of the sport. In 1968, kicking directly into touch from outside the twenty-five yard line was prohibited, which was to have a significant effect on keeping the ball in play for longer. The attraction of the game for spectators was further developed in 1971, when the value of a try was increased to four points. In 1967, Wales became the first country to adopt a national coaching and squad system, which helped develop tactical play and thinking in the national and club game. Most significantly, these developments coincided with the emergence of a new generation of Welsh players of extraordinary talent and breathtaking flair. The ground was set for a heady period of intoxicating success.

Between 1968–9 and 1978–9, Wales won the Five Nations Championship six times, collecting three grand slams and six triple crowns in the process. The gulf between Wales and the other home nations became clear in 1971, when Wales won its first grand slam for nineteen years and supplied thirteen players for the British Lions' successful tour of New Zealand. The captain was London Welsh's John Dawes and the coach Llanelli's Carwyn James. In the first test, there were ten Welshmen in the Lions side. The Welsh sides of the 1970s were not quite as dominant as many nostalgic memories suggest but they were certainly as entertaining. The standard of backplay excited fans and journalists alike and drew parallels with the 'total football' played by the famous Dutch soccer sides of the 1970s. Players such as J. P. R. Williams, who added a whole new attacking dimension to full-back play, and winger Gerald Davies, with his scorching speed and sidesteps, became the envy of the rugby world. True to their history, the selectors did not always fully appreciate the talents at their disposal and Phil Bennett, another of the era's greats, was not always first choice for his country, much to the disgust of fans from Llanelli. Perhaps the greatest player of the century, let alone the 1970s, was the son of a miner from Gwaun-cae-Gurwen in the Welsh-speaking coalfield on the edge of Glamorgan. Gareth Edwards's explosive running and breadth of passing astounded and delighted fans, critics and opposing teams alike. He retired in 1978, the most capped Welshman ever and with a shared record for the number of tries. Such exciting backs still needed solid forwards of course and in the Pontypool front row (Bobby Windsor, Charlie Faulkner and Graham Price) they found a formidable but mobile base. Meanwhile, number eight Mervyn Davies gave the Welsh team not only its most capped forward to that date, but also a swerving lynchpin in both attack and defence. By the late 1970s, new talents were emerging to replace the ageing stars. Players such as Steve Fenwick and Ray Gravell may not have been as spectacular but the team remained as successful and Wales finished the decade with four consecutive triple crowns. Why so many talented players emerged at once remains a matter of conjecture. The WRU naturally pointed to the success of its coaching and youth initiatives; a popular Max Boyce song spoke of an outside half factory built beneath a south Wales mountain. Although not always acknowledged, seen or appreciated, schoolteachers certainly played an important role. From a love of the game, many teachers devoted considerable time, in and out of school, to helping develop young players of ability.[2] There was also undoubtedly an element of chance in Wales's fortune but success breeds success and the Welsh XVs of the 1970s acted as an inspiration to many budding players.

The grandeur on the pitch was matched by the surroundings of Cardiff Arms Park, which was rebuilt in the 1960s and divided into two: a Welsh National Stadium with concrete arms reaching out above the river Taff to cradle the new seats, and a separate club ground for Cardiff RFC on the old cricket pitch. The main pitch may have improved without the burden of regular club games but the project left the WRU with a heavy debt. Financing was helped by debentures that guaranteed their purchasers an opportunity to buy the match tickets that were now even more elusive than ever. Players often felt under extreme pressure regarding who they should allocate their tickets to, and the lengths Welshmen would go to secure a ticket became the subject of jokes and folklore. For those lucky enough to get in, the national stadium became a Welsh Mecca, adorned on matchdays with red rosettes, giant leeks and daffodils, and ringing to the sound of hymns and 'Oggi-Oggi-Oggi, Oi-Oi-Oi', a new invented tradition by former miner and poet/performer Max Boyce. Both players and spectators held the new stadium and its acoustics in special affection and to many it was 'the rugby shrine of the world'.[3] The Arms Park's role as a focal point for rugby, to which people descended from across Wales, contributed to a growth in the acceptance of Cardiff as the capital city that it had been belatedly declared to be in 1955.[4] Welsh fans also continued to travel to away fixtures *en masse*, often saving for the trip with weekly contributions as they had begun to do before the Second World War. The alcoholic and parochial excitement of these excursions to the cosmopolitan centres of London, Dublin, Paris and Edinburgh was captured brilliantly in Boyce's song *Hymns and Arias*.[5] This mix of beer, song and sex was the continuation of an inter-war tradition that had seen Welsh miners head to Cardiff for matches followed by 'ale and chops and tarts'.[6]

The impact of the national XV's victories went far beyond those watching in the stadium. With interest bolstered by a patriotic media and regular victories, television now enabled internationals to become a regular national event that embraced areas outside the game's traditional hinterlands. For four Saturday afternoons a year, rugby seemed to bring much of Wales to a standstill, as it won the interest of even those for whom sport was a marginal aside at all other times. The social base of the game was broadening and, in tune with the liberating ethos of the day, there were more women following and watching rugby from the late 1960s (although others, such as my mother, took advantage of the fact that the shops were quiet on international days). Even in north Wales, there was a new passion for the game emerging and new clubs such as Bala and Bethesda were formed. Meanwhile, in the south, clubhouses continued to develop as social (and drinking) centres for local communities, replacing, in some places, the old miners' and welfare institutes that were declining with the traditional industries that had spawned them. It was in this world of second-class rugby, complete with its chauvinism, jealousies, friendships and passionate local pride, that the lifeblood that fed the international game could be found.

As in the past, the players at the heart of the international fanaticism were very much rooted in Welsh culture. A mixture of English and Welsh speakers and a combination of manual workers and the products of grammar schools: they were a reflection of the nation they represented. The number of teachers, students, doctors and other public sector workers was on the increase, as industrial Wales slipped into terminal decline. The developing importance of professional men for Welsh rugby, as well as the pull the British capital continued to exert on the young and ambitious of Wales, was symbolized by the emergence of London Welsh RFC as a regular source of players for the national side in the late 1960s and early 1970s.[7] J. P. R. Williams, a London medical student and instantly recognizable by his initials and fashionably long sideburns, was the most famous of the London Welsh players. He felt that he and the other Welsh stars were treated like royalty. Women and girls even curtsied to Barry John. The King, as John was often known, was a fly half whose almost casual talents with the ball made rugby look graceful. His running was fast, swerving and powerful and he was seemingly able to place the ball where he liked, whether between the posts or into touch. The Welsh public loved him for it but the fame and constant attention was too much. He was the product of a Welsh-speaking west Wales mining family but, like George Best, with whom he found much in common, John felt deified and as if he were living in a 'goldfish bowl'. He retired prematurely to regain his freedom and privacy.[8] Current soccer stars are able to escape such attention by the physical and emotional distance that their wealth puts between them and their fans. But the Welsh rugby stars of the 1970s were amateurs, still mostly working and living in Wales, and this kept them rooted in the society that worshipped them. Edwards, John, Gerald Davies and many of the other stars were the sons of manual workers but who themselves had, through education, gone into white-collar careers. Yet, even in this, they could be seen as symbolic of Wales's long-established regard for education and social progress. Hand in hand with this regard had always been the importance of never forgetting one's roots, something that amateurism and the adoration of Wales ensured its rugby heroes never did.

Despite rugby's amateur status, the material rewards for playing seemed to be on the increase. Early in his career, when Barry John played for a police team, supporters would have a collection to raise pocket money for him.[9] Many smaller clubs made direct cash payments to their players to prevent them from being lured away. When players did switch clubs, financial inducements were certainly not uncommon. Unknown or overlooked by the game's authorities, some of the star players of the 1970s received cash payments for wearing the boots of various manufacturers. The bigger teams, such as Cardiff RFC, refused to make financial transactions but offered rewards in kind such as easy jobs and, with the help of local firms, free cars, clothing and meals. Rugby certainly opened doors for players to new occupations in business and consultancy, where the fame of rugby was attractive to both employer and customer. People wanted to be associated with the best players, which also meant that there were free meals, drinks and holidays to be enjoyed. Such material benefits helped the stars resist the financial lure of rugby league. But they were also kept at home by the promise of playing success, by strong personal attachments to Wales and their local communities and by pressure from within those communities. Similarly, Llanelli RFC tried to keep Barry John from signing for Cardiff RFC by appealing to his sense of history and tradition. The professional game remained a threat however. Even in the confident 1970s, former union heroes could be asked to leave their local clubhouses after they had gone north. As the proverb went, there were three things best not discussed in polite Welsh society: politics, religion and rugby league.

The rugby authorities, of course, forbade direct payments to players. After retirement there was the legal possibility of an autobiography, journalism and personal appearances but by then the fame of most stars was subsiding and many sought that route whilst at their playing peak. Thus amateurism in rugby became not a question of if you were paid but rather of how you were paid. The sport's authorities themselves were also becoming more commercial. In 1969, a Sunday-afternoon rugby highlights programme began on the BBC, allowing the club game to reach a much broader audience and develop the potential for sponsorship and the advertising hoardings that began to appear at club and international grounds from the mid-1970s. And yet the game still remained amateur in a very real sense. Players were still going to work the day before an international, and many were reliant on goodwilled employers to secure time to play, train and tour. Rugby may not have been strictly amateur but professionalism remained a long way off.

Rugby union certainly fell behind soccer in taking advantage of the commercial opportunities that television and sponsorship offered. From the 1960s, unofficial club championships, calculated by newspapers, were encouraged by rugby clubs in order to attract spectators but opportunities to introduce an official Welsh league were missed. In 1977, the WRU Challenge Cup became the Schweppes Cup, but it was another two years before its final was live on television. It was not until 1974 that the WRU sanctioned club games on the Sabbath, an overdue symbol of the crumbling influence of Nonconformity in Wales. The Welsh club game was not a haven of forward thinking but it did enjoy something of a golden period in the 1970s. Nowhere was this clearer than in October 1972, when the Stradey Park scoreboard proudly declared 'Llanelli 9 Seland Newydd 3'. The defeat of the All Blacks before a boisterous crowd of nearly 24,000 people was no fluke and owed much to the coaching of Carwyn James. There were six internationals in the Llanelli team, as well as another three players who would be capped in the future. In short, Llanelli was the outstanding club team of the late 1960s and early 1970s, although many in Pontypool would have passionately disputed that in the first half of the seventies, as rugby continued to be a source of intense local patriotism.

Later in the 1972–3 All Blacks tour, Gareth Edwards scored a try for the Barbarians that encapsulated the brilliance of the

Welsh running game and provided television with a piece of footage that is still frequently repeated. British press coverage of such play, and Welsh rugby in general, drew heavily on certain national stereotypes but it also helped to dispel others. The Welsh XVs were described as 'magical', 'poetic', 'rhythmic', 'shrewd' and 'fighters'.[10] No longer were Taffy and his kin seen, in the words of historian John Davies, as 'puritan chapel-goers but rather as muscular boozers who were doubtful whether there was life beyond the dead-ball line'.[11] Many of the players themselves thought that rugby reflected the Celtic and emotional temperament of the Welsh. Barry John saw rugby as 'tough and fast, a man's game with its own controlled violence, its special skills and lore, its combination of brain and muscle, the emotional involvement of watchers and watched, [it] has always appealed strongly to the Welsh temperament'.[12] Such alleged national characteristics may have only been grounded in a distinctly limited reality but they formed part of a very real patriotism. Players spoke of their pride in donning the Welsh shirt and coaches appealed to such sentiments in trying to raise their game. Richard Holt has speculated that the sense of Welshness may have been particularly sharp for those players who made the break from the world of manual labour 'with its fierce solidarities and sense of place'.[13] In 1977, captain Phil Bennett rallied his team-mates before a match by declaring: 'These English you're just going out to meet have taken our coal, our water, our steel: they buy our houses and live in them a fortnight a year . . . Down the centuries these English have exploited and pillaged us – and we're playing them this afternoon boys'.[14]

The 1960s had seen a growth in political national consciousness in Wales. A Welsh Office and Secretary of State for Wales had been created in 1964, whilst in 1966 the nationalist party Plaid Cymru won its first parliamentary seat. The party's subsequent gradual growth in support, alongside Labour's own desire for more effective and sensitive governance for Wales, created pressure for a more revolutionary measure of devolution. Alongside this were the more radical but marginal campaigns of *Cymdeithas yr Iaith* (the Welsh Language Society) and the Free Wales Army. The former campaigned for greater recognition and use of the Welsh language, with tactics that included obliterating English-only roadsigns; the latter flirted with bombs and military uniforms in its inept campaign for a Welsh republic. Thus, as with many liberal causes worldwide, the 1960s began a new, more pronounced and concerted era for Welsh national consciousness. Rugby both contributed to and reflected this. As Smith and Williams point out, rugby internationals became 'more overtly nationalistic', with Free Wales Army T-shirts visible in the crowd and the concerted booing of the *God Save the Queen*. This new world upset some of the conservative older generation, as did the decline in hymn singing at internationals which was often blamed on the demolition of the old North Enclosure.[15] Tom Jones's *Delilah* and the Max Boyce songs that often replaced the hymns may not have been as religious or as traditional but they were more representative of the modernist, innovative and commercial popular culture of the 1960s and 1970s. Yet rugby in this period was also seen by some as a safety valve for such nationalistic sentiments.[16] The failure of the 1979 referendum on devolution certainly signalled the limitations of Welsh political identity. For all the popular pride in Wales, it could not be equated with a widespread desire for political autonomy.

II

The 1980s were a period of dramatic change for Wales. Thatcherism's commitment to the free market spelt the death knell for the traditional heavy industries on which modern Wales had been built. Mines and steelworks disappeared to be replaced by rising unemployment and scattered modernist ventures, such as Japanese electronics factories that employed as many women as men. In 1981, there were 27,000 miners in Wales; by 1990, there was just one working pit in Wales. By the mid 1980s in some former mining communities in Mid Glamorgan, as many as one in three 16 to 19-year-old men were on the dole. As in the inter-war period, rugby seemed to reflect this economic downturn.[17] The sustained glories of the 1970s were not repeated and the 1980s were largely a dismal period for Welsh rugby. In 1981, as the Welsh Rugby Union celebrated its centenary, there were worrying signs of what lay ahead. A comprehensive 34–18 defeat by Scotland ended a run of 27 home championship games without defeat. A 23–3 thrashing by New Zealand was Wales's heaviest home defeat for ninety-eight years. Rugby's first ever world cup, held in Australia and New Zealand in 1987, seemed to offer Welsh rugby some hope. Wales secured third place but it proved to be a false dawn, as anyone who looked at the 49–6 hammering by New Zealand in the semi-final could tell. There was a triple crown in 1988 but performances were resting too much on the shoulders of the talented Jonathan Davies. He went north in 1989 and there were no more consecutive victories until 1994. In 1990 and 1991, Wales failed to win a single Five Nations match and England won at the Arms Park for the first time since 1963. Worse was to come in the 1991 World Cup when even Western Samoa inflicted a home defeat on the Welsh.

Many saw the seeds of the decline in rugby's grassroots. Gwendraeth grammar school had produced Carwyn James, Barry John, Gareth Davies and Jonathan Davies, a world-class outside half a decade. Trials for the school side would be attended by hundreds of boys and the school's achievements and fanaticism for rugby summed up how the sport was ingrained in the culture of Welsh education, much to the cost of Welsh soccer. But in the 1980s, Gwendraeth grammar went comprehensive and the place and nature of school sport changed (as it did across Britain). Teachers' voluntary extra-curricular involvement in physical education lessened, at least partly in protest at the Thatcher government's management of education. Physical education itself diversified as games and activities such as basketball and dance lessened the emphasis on competitive sports. Outside school, with video games, BMX bikes, skateboards and other new forms of globalized entertainment, there emerged a greater diversity of sporting and leisure interests amongst both boys and teachers. The net result was a more varied and cosmopolitan Welsh popular culture, where rugby occupied a more peripheral place and even Gwendraeth's first XV ceased to exist for a period. The school was not unique and, as other Welsh grammars disappeared, were amalgamated or changed, a cog in the conveyor belt of Welsh rugby was removed.[18]

The 1980s and 1990s were a period of realignment for Wales. The economy awkwardly adapted to make the most of foreign inward investment. The national curriculum for Wales, S4C (the Welsh television channel) and a second Welsh Language Act seemed to secure the future of the language, and the Labour Party and Plaid Cymru redefined their programmes to adapt to a modern world and the debacle of the 1979 referendum. Such changes were often accompanied by emotional and political arguments over whether they represented pragmatic adaptation or philosophical betrayals. Attempts to restructure Welsh rugby also brought similar dilemmas but with less success. After years of argument, it was not until 1990 that the much-needed national league was introduced. Such lack of vision in the game's hierarchy, the poor performances on the pitch and the weak Welsh economy encouraged a new glut of defections to rugby league. In 1985, Terry Holmes became the first leading Welsh player to head north for over a decade. A third of the 1988 triple crown team were lost to the professional game and there was a new threat at home with the Cardiff Blue Dragons rugby league club playing at Ninian Park from 1981 until 1984. The biggest loss was Jonathan Davies, who joined Widnes for a record fee of almost £200,000, disillusioned, like so many, at the management of the Welsh game.[19] Despite the obvious reasons to go, the players who did leave were often accused of profiteering or treachery. Scott Gibbs, on joining St Helen's from Swansea, said: 'It grates me that I am called a prostitute while players and officials keep on covering up what's going on in union. Every player in Wales knows that when you play on a Saturday, if you win you can get a few quid. Players get the cash after the game.'[20] In this wider climate of change and uncertainty, the definitions of amateurism were growing even more elastic and more vulnerable. The fear of being exposed may have prevented some players from taking all they could but the desire to be open in their earnings continued to be an incentive for Welshmen to head north.

An amateur sport with a television following of millions was increasingly becoming an anachronism by the 1990s. With many UK players working in business, they recognized the commercial potential of rugby and called for a modernization of the limits on players' earnings. By the early 1990s, rugby administrators were complaining that players were holding clubs to ransom for 'cars, cash and jobs'.[21] But the final catalyst for change was Rupert Murdoch's decision to pump money into rugby league. Soccer had already been transformed by Sky Television's millions and a similar pump priming in the league code threatened to take players, sponsorship and even fans away from the union game. When professionalization came in 1995, it was shockingly sudden, as a century of history was wiped away with a single decision. Welsh rugby thus entered the modern, arguably post-industrial, era on the coat-tails of change elsewhere.

The new professional era in Welsh rugby was also signalled by the appointment of New Zealander Graham Henry as coach in 1998. Henry began selecting players whose Welsh heritage was remote and sometimes somewhat dubious. Although this rankled with some purists, it was inevitable if Wales wanted to compete with the cream of the world's rugby nations. As in club soccer, success was more important than the national heritage of the players who achieved it. However, the policy backfired in the 'Grannygate scandal', when the Welsh ancestry of capped players Shane Howarth and Brett Sinkinson, both from New Zealand, was proved false. Under Henry, dubbed the Great Redeemer, renaissances on the field came and went but they did not discredit those who felt that the standards of play and organization in Welsh rugby were too low. Nonetheless, the false dawn of 1999 was particularly sweet, with an exciting victory over France in Paris and then a last gasp defeat of England at Wembley, courtesy of a surging try by Scott Gibbs and a Neil Jenkins conversion. Jenkins himself was a kicker of the ball good enough to grace the Welsh teams of the 1970s but he was never fully appreciated in a period when self-doubt and argument riddled the Welsh game. The impact of the professionalism on the domestic game was profound uncertainty and change as clubs and the WRU struggled to make the financial transition. The 1998–9 season was one of acrimony, writs and near farce, with Cardiff and Swansea RFCs preferring to play friendlies against English sides rather than compete in a Welsh league. Both clubs returned to the domestic fold but there continued to be pressure for British and European competitions in the hope of raising standards and attendances. The pressure for a radical overhaul was increased by the WRU having to step in to financially save leading clubs like Llanelli and Neath. In 2003, the eventual outcome of various experimental configurations was a two-tier system of five regional teams playing in a Celtic league with a national Welsh Premiership below them in which clubs retained their separate identities. The regional teams, formed by forcibly amalgamating some clubs but leaving others, had a controversial beginning with arguments over names, money and player ownership. The situation was complicated when Pontypridd RFC went bankrupt and the WRU axed the (Pontypridd–Bridgend) Celtic Warriors regional team. This left the regions as the Cardiff Blues, Neath–Swansea Ospreys, Newport Gwent Dragons and Llanelli Scarlets. Three of these teams did not seem to be regions at all but rather old clubs now entitled to take players from their neighbours for Celtic league matches. Whatever the doubts, standards seemed to rise which helped Wales win an unexpected but very exciting grand slam in 2005, its first since 1978.

III

Rugby triumphs meant that Welsh soccer was often over-shadowed in both the Welsh and British media. Yet it continued to be an integral part of Welsh popular culture, as both a participatory and spectator sport, throughout the entire post-war period. The 1960s saw a revolution in the game, thanks to the 1961 abolition of the maximum wage. For the great Welsh players of the 1950s and 1960s, this change came too late and none of them made their fortunes from soccer. In Italy, John Charles earned far in excess of what he would have done in England but his family missed home and he returned to play for Leeds in 1962. He had lost his pace and had personal problems and was soon consoling himself with alcohol and playing for Hereford United. By 1988, Charles was reduced to the ignominy of a short imprisonment because of unpaid taxes.[22]

Even as televised football became increasingly prominent in the broadcasting schedules of the 1960s, none of the Welsh sides established themselves as leading British clubs and thus they were unable to retain or attract the cream of the domestic talent. Swansea Town did reach a FA Cup semi-final in 1964 but lost to Preston North End. In the late 1970s and early 1980s, the club enjoyed a rollercoaster ride under player-manager John Toshack, which saw it promoted from the fourth division to the first in just four seasons. Toshack had been a lynchpin of the all-conquering Liverpool team of the mid-1970s and he was able to augment a number of highly gifted local youngsters, such as Robbie James and Alan Curtis, with highly experienced English players nearing the end of their careers. The Swans finished sixth in their exhilarating first season (1981–2) in the top flight but had spent heavily on new players in the process. It was a short-lived success: injury and financial and management problems then brought two consecutive relegations. In 1986, the club was declared bankrupt, before being saved by a local businessman. Subsequent years saw the club languishing in the lower divisions, although in 2000 Swansea did win the third division championship. Yet, less than two years later, the club was again on the brink of financial collapse and far removed from the riches of the Premiership. Survival was secured, partly thanks to the establishment of a Supporters' Trust, as fans realized that they needed to take financial action if small clubs were to survive in a marketplace dominated by teams that were glamorous and successful. The financial demands of competing in that marketplace also led to the club moving to a new 20,000 seated stadium in 2005, to be shared with the regional rugby side the Ospreys, and where ticket prices and sponsor opportunities were increased. Departing from the Vetch and St Helen's was a source of sadness to most fans, for whom sports grounds held strong emotional attachments. Yet the virtual absence of voices of objection to the move signalled supporters' belief that in sport progress matters more than history.

As a young striker with his hometown club, John Toshack was also involved with boosting Cardiff City's fortunes on and off the pitch. He left for Liverpool midseason in 1970 for a then staggering £110,000. City was sitting at the top of the second division, but after the sale of its 21-year-old star striker, results faltered and the club missed out on promotion. There was considerable anger amongst fans who accused the club, not for the first or last time, of lacking ambition. The club's last stay in the top flight had been brief (1960–2) but it did find some consistency in the Welsh Cup which it won ten times in the 1960s and 1970s. In 1964, the winners of the Welsh Cup were granted entry to the European Cup Winners Cup. This enabled a number of memorable European runs for Welsh clubs. In 1968, Cardiff City reached the competition's semi-finals where it lost to SV Hamburg. In 1971, helped perhaps by deliberately turning off the heating in the away team's dressing room,[23] second-division Cardiff City beat Real Madrid 1–0 at Ninian Park in front of 47,500. Although it lost the second leg 2–0, the result stands as one of the club's greatest ever moments.

Wrexham FC has also enjoyed its biggest moments in cup competitions. In 1976, it reached the quarter-finals of the Cup Winners Cup, losing to Anderlecht, the eventual winners. The club reached the FA Cup quarter-finals in 1974, 1978 and 1997, while, in 1992, having finished bottom of the fourth division the previous season, Wrexham knocked league champions Arsenal out of the competition. But, apart from a brief period in the old second division (1978–82), the club has remained rooted in the league's bottom two divisions. Soccer continued to marginalize rugby as the most popular spectator sport in north Wales but, perhaps discouraged by Wrexham's lack of success, many of the region's football fans pledged their allegiances to the nearby success and glamour of Liverpool and Everton. The biggest symbol in Wales of the divide in popularity and wealth within British football was at Newport County. Although it reached the quarter-finals of the European Cup Winners Cup in 1980–1, the financially stricken club was relegated from the Football League in 1988 and closed down a year later.

The coverage in national tabloids and the steady growth of football on the radio ensured that the English first division already attracted strong interest in Wales by the 1950s, but television now meant that English soccer was fully accessible to a Welsh audience that had not lost its British loyalties. The 1966 World Cup was enjoyed across Wales and a *Western Mail* editorial proclaimed England's 'superb victory' as an achievement that 'the whole of Britain can feel proud of' and which 'belongs to British football as a whole'.[24] In the 1990s, saturation television coverage and the new fashionability of football furthered the passionate support within Wales for leading English clubs, much to the detriment of the domestic Welsh game. By 2001, there were twelve official branches of the Manchester United Supporters' Club across Wales, spread out as far as Aberystwyth and Pontypridd.[25] Although it has given small Welsh towns a route to European football and recognition, the national League of Wales, set up in 1992, has not really been a popular success. In 2001–2, average attendances stood at around 280,[26] a very low figure compared to the three Welsh clubs that play in the English Football League. These clubs, like their fans and three other leading Welsh teams, remain vehemently opposed to joining their national league. The importance of sponsorship to contemporary sport was particularly evident in the League of Wales. The prolonged lack of a league sponsor meant the competition lacked credibility in many eyes, while Llansantffraid and Inter Cardiff took the radical step of re-naming their teams after the companies that sponsored them. Hooliganism was another reason why some have been reluctant to accept soccer as a Welsh sport. Cardiff City and Swansea City fans both have, at least partially deserved, reputations for hooliganism. Crowd disorder and violence has a long history in both rugby and soccer,[27] but the existence of gangs of youths who went to games looking for trouble was a new development of the 1960s. By the 1980s, matches between the two clubs were blighted by serious trouble, causing away fans to be banned from the derbies between 1993 and 1997. Despite Welsh soccer's commitment to the English game, the fans remain strongly, often crudely, and occasionally violently, loyal to Wales. Anti-English chanting and Welsh flags are very much a feature of Welsh club football, and games in the Football League are injected with something of the flavour of the international contest.

Welsh players employed in England have also retained their sense of patriotism. In Ian Rush and Mark Hughes, Wales produced two of the Britain's greatest post-war strikers. Rush, from Flintshire, was a highly successful goal poacher with the great Liverpool teams of the 1980s. His talents led to a £3.2 million transfer to Juventus of Italy but he failed to settle, notoriously remarking that it was like being in a foreign country. He returned to Liverpool in 1987 to resume his punishment of first-division defences and break the record for the number of international goals by a Welshman. Mark Hughes, another north Walian and a more spectacular but less potent goal machine than Rush, also enjoyed a brief and largely unhappy period abroad with Barcelona and Bayern Munich. But it was with Manchester United, during the autumn of his career and the beginning of the club's 1990s domination of English football, that he enjoyed the most success. The Manchester United of the 1990s was embodied perfectly in Ryan Giggs, born in Cardiff but raised in Manchester after his father moved there to join Swinton rugby league club. His good looks, dazzling pace and ball skills made Giggs an excellent pin up and footballer. When he burst into the United first team as a precocious seventeen-year-old winger, the parallels with George Best were quick to come. However, protected by the media nous of his club and manager, Giggs avoided the chaotic glamour that enveloped Best or Barry John. Instead, he settled down to play brilliant football and earn his fortune. By 2001, he was worth an estimated £10 million, making him the sixth-equal richest sports star in the UK and the richest in Wales.[28] Giggs's appearances for his country have been significantly limited by injuries (although many fans suspected that some were invented by Sir Alex Ferguson) but, when he has played, he has not inspired any general revival in the national team's fortunes. The few world-class players Wales has produced have been forced to play alongside a succession of mediocre journeymen. This has denied them the opportunity to perform in the finals of international tournaments and ensured soccer's continued marginalization in media depictions of Welsh sporting culture.

Had the national team enjoyed any real success then fans' complaints of a Welsh media bias towards the oval ball might have been proved wrong. In 1976, there was a brief moment of success when Wales qualified for the quarter-finals of the European Championship, then played on a home-and-away basis. After losing the away leg 2–0 to Yugoslavia, the return game at Ninian Park was marred by crowd trouble when Welsh fans invaded the pitch and threw cans after the referee had disallowed a Welsh goal. Wales saw a further goal disallowed and a penalty saved before their progress in the competition was finally at an end. In other qualifying competitions everything seemed to conspire against Wales at times. In 1981, a floodlight failure saw Wales lose their concentration and throw away what should have been a crucial win against Iceland in their final qualifier. In 1978 and 1985, controversial penalties against Wales saw Scotland secure crucial victories that helped secure qualification. Wales's disappointment in the latter game was overshadowed by the death of the Scottish manager Jock Stein, who never recovered after collapsing at the end of the game. Perhaps Wales's closest brush with qualification was for the 1994 World Cup. As well as Hughes and Rush, the team also had defensive rocks in Neville Southall and Kevin Ratcliffe. Although perhaps past their peak by the early 1990s, both had played for the great Everton side of the mid-1980s that enjoyed league and European success. Southall was a keeper of huge stature who won a record 92 Welsh caps. To qualify for the 1994 World Cup, Wales needed to beat Romania in its final game. With the score at 1–1, a stunned Arms Park crowd watched Paul Bodin crash a penalty against the Romanian crossbar. The chance was gone and Wales went on to lose 2–1. After the game, the contract of Terry Yorath, the Welsh manager who himself was a former international of some repute, was controversially not renewed. The FAW and Welsh team then seemed to enter into a period of farce. John Toshack resigned after just forty-seven days as national manager, hinting at behind-the-scenes skullduggery. He was succeeded by Mike Smith and then Bobby Gould, who presided over a significant decline in both performances and respect for the national team. By 2000, Mark Hughes himself was the national manager and things were looking brighter but despite some much improved performances qualification was as elusive as ever. Hughes quit in 2004 to take charge of Blackburn Rovers, an indication of the position of the Welsh national team in football's contemporary pecking order.

IV

In 1968, Swansea witnessed a piece of cricketing history when Gary Sobers hit six sixes in a single over for Nottinghamshire against Glamorgan.[29] Despite being on the receiving end of this thumping, the end of the 1960s did see Welsh sporting success on the cricket field. In 1969, Glamorgan CCC secured the county championship for the second time in its history. Ironically, its best of player of the decade, bowler Jeff Jones who appeared in fifteen tests for England, had retired the previous year after injury. The championship was secured by a team that consisted of a number of all-rounders: eight of the main first XI took wickets during the season. Included in that number was Majid Khan, the club's designated overseas player and one of the most graceful batsmen of his generation. He spent nine years with Glamorgan and played sixty-three tests for Pakistan. The captain of the 1969 championship side was Tony Lewis, a Cambridge graduate from Neath and an effective middle-order batsman. He was capped nine times in 1972–3 and remains the only Glamorgan player to captain England in a test match. Lewis scored 20,495 first-class runs before injury forced him to retire in 1974. He then embarked on a highly influential career as broadcaster, journalist and administrator. Although Glamorgan finished runners-up in the 1970 championship, the club endured a largely dismal period until the 1990s, with an appearance in the final of the 1977 Gillette Cup being a rare bright moment. There were, however, some talented players. Matthew Maynard, Hugh Morris, Greg Thomas and Steve Watkin were all Welshmen and long-serving Glamorgan players who enjoyed brief England careers. In 1990, things began to look up when Viv Richards joined after a highly successful career with the West Indies and Somerset. He was one of the world's all-time greats, who inspired his team-mates, pulled in the crowds and was fundamental to the club winning the Sunday League championship in 1993.

Glamorgan were as much representatives of Wales as they were of a county that was actually abolished in 1974. When, in 1964, Glamorgan beat Australia for the first time, the *Western Mail* exclaimed 'What a moment of triumph for Wales', while the 7,000 'crowd gathered round the pavilion and solemnly sang the national anthem in thanks for a great victory'.[30] The county's unofficial national status was enhanced by the club having no fixed home. In the post-war years it has played regular home games in Cardiff, Swansea, Abergavenny, Newport,

Neath, Pontypridd, Ebbw Vale, Llanelli and even Colwyn Bay in the north. After the redevelopment of the Arms Park in 1967, Glamorgan CCC made Sophia Gardens its Cardiff base and developed the facilities there to include an indoor school. Such long-term investment paid off when Glamorgan secured the county championship in 1997. At the heart of the success was Steve James, whose 1,775 runs made him the country's leading run score in first-class cricket. Matthew Maynard and Hugh Morris were the other batting stalwarts, while Waqar Younis took sixty-eight wickets that season adding a new bite to the team's bowling. The other mainstay of the team's bowling was Robert Croft, an effective spinner who never quite managed to produce the same level of consistency when selected for England.[31]

The amateur-professional distinction in cricket was abolished in 1962, as the game struggled to modernize and fit in with the less overtly class-based society of the post-war years. One day matches, sponsored trophies, Sunday leagues and even floodlit games saw the sport revolutionized in the quest to maintain its popularity and increase its income. Driving these changes was the promise of television and associated commercial revenues. Television has undoubtedly been the most significant influence on sport in the post-war years. As well as the obvious enrichment of soccer in the post-1992 Premiership age, other sports such as snooker have been completely overhauled by television coverage. After the invention of colour television, snooker was featured on the BBC from the late 1960s and the sport became something of a 'national obsession'.[32] The relatively static nature of the game meant that it was cheap to broadcast and conducive to dramatic close ups. The sport of course had a much longer history in Wales and beyond thanks to tables in welfare halls and pubs. Former collier, Ray Reardon, world champion six times in the 1970s, learnt to play snooker in the Miners' Institute in Tredegar in the 1930s. With television coverage highlighting the different personalities, quirks and traits of the players, the likes of Reardon and Terry Griffiths (the 1979 world champion who hailed from Llanelli) became wealthy celebrities as well as sports stars. Doug Mountjoy, another former Welsh miner and world amateur champion in 1976, won £500,000 in a career that saw him in the world top sixteen for eleven years. With such players, Wales won the snooker world cup in 1979 and 1980. Television coverage of the sport led to a dramatic increase in the number of people playing snooker both in Wales and Britain as a whole. The size and cost of snooker tables prevented many players from buying their own but snooker halls enjoyed a new-found popularity, although their smoky and beery environment narrowed the potential clientele. As fashion moved on, snooker lost some of its popularity in the 1990s but a new generation of Welsh players emerged at the top of the game. Mark Williams was runner up in the world championship in 1999 and winner in 2000, when he beat Matthew Stevens in an all-Welsh final. Other sports were also revolutionized by television. Darts was taken from the smoky pub to the lucrative television screen but it still retained its firmly working-class character. In 1978, Leighton Rees of Ynys-y-Bwl won the inaugural world darts championship and its prize of £300. A former factory worker, he developed his darts in working-men's clubs and pubs where his 'interest and dedication' was captured by the 'terrific social deal'. He did not turn professional until 1976, when he was 36 years old and the new levels of sponsorship in the televised game suddenly made a career in darts a realistic possibility. Even then, the decision to take the risk of giving up his job was a difficult one.[33]

A more lucrative profession was golf, which television took into the realms of a truly global sport. With sponsorship revenue growing in the 1950s, tensions emerged within the sport between the traditional and hierarchical instincts of the administrators and the meritocratic and commercial demands of the star professionals. As the past and future collided, a Welshman, Dai Rees, emerged as a key progressive force in revolutionizing the old-school-tie-and-blazer Professional Golfers' Association, which viewed professionals as skilled artisans employed to coach club members.[34] Rees was born in Barry but moved to Aberdare as a youngster where his father was the local golf club's professional. In 1957, aged 44, he captained the Ryder Cup team that won the title for Europe for the first time in 22 years. The success brought him considerable fame and Rees won the 1957 BBC Sports Personality award, the only Welshman ever to do so. In the 1980s, another Welsh golfer emerged who would become world-class and take full advantage of the riches that Rees had helped secure for tour players. Ian Woosnam was actually from Oswestry, a town just over the English border, but his parents were Welsh and he too considered himself Welsh. Woosnam won the 1991 US Masters and 29 European PGA Tour titles, and was the leading money winner on the European Tour in 1987 and 1990. In 1991, he topped the world rankings and by the end of 2001 he had earned nearly £8 million during his career. The scale of such earnings signified just how big a part sponsorship played in sport by the 1990s. Thanks to Woosnam and others Wales was gaining some significance in the golfing world. In 1987, he had partnered David Llewellyn to win the World Cup for Wales. By 2001, the PGA's list of the top 100 golfers in Europe had seven Welshmen in it. This meant that Wales had one European Tour player for every 209,542 persons, a ratio greater than any other country on the continent.[35] Wales's stature in the golfing world was further demonstrated by the selection of Newport's Celtic Manor complex for the 2010 Ryder Cup tournament. Actual participation in golf also seemed to be rising and the 1990s saw 67 new courses open in Wales, taking the national total to 201. Yet this did not signal a complete democratization of the game. Over half of Welsh clubs remained members-only, with some having a three-year waiting list for membership.[36]

Despite its television coverage, boxing's integral place in Welsh popular culture subsided with the industrial culture that had first spawned its popularity. There was no modern-day equivalent of the widely popular Jimmy Driscoll or Freddie Welsh but there were Welsh boxers of considerable talent. Merthyr, a depressed town struggling to come to terms with an economy where coal was in severe decline, was particularly proud of three famous fighters it produced. In 1951, Eddie Thomas held British, Empire and European titles at welterweight. He subsequently managed Howard Winstone who won gold at the 1958 Empire Games and went on to become world featherweight champion in 1968. Symbolic perhaps of the wider conditions from which these men came, Winstone had had to overcome the loss of the top of three of his fingers in an industrial accident. Johnny Owen was a skinny, endurable and hugely popular bantamweight. He won the Commonwealth and European titles but, in 1980, he was knocked out in a world title bout in Los Angeles. Owen was taken to hospital in a coma and died two weeks later. He was 24 years old. Such casualties raised public questions about the ethics of a sport built on violence but Welsh boxers have enjoyed more success in recent years despite this growing condemnation of their sport. Steve Robinson of Cardiff was WBO world feather-weight champion from 1993 to 1995. Robbie Regan became world flyweight champion in 1995 and world bantamweight champion in 1996. In 1997, Joe Calzaghe of Newbridge beat Chris Eubank to win the WBO super middleweight championship of the world. Yet, by the end of the twentieth century, such boxing champions were associated with a global, commercial and glamorous sporting culture that was far removed from the Wales of men such as Eddie Thomas and his industrial Merthyr.

If there was a sport that encapsulated the global commercial sporting culture of the end of the century, it was ice hockey. The first ice hockey team in Wales was formed in Deeside in 1974 but it was the Cardiff Devils, formed in 1986, that was to give the sport a high profile in Wales. Based at the new Welsh National Ice-rink, the club quickly moved up through the sport's league structure, attracting crowds of several thousand in the process. The Devils won the Heineken League first division in 1989 and then the premier division in 1990. It went on to become one of the most successful teams in UK ice hockey, winning every domestic honour available. However, employing north American stars was expensive and, after a period of controversial ownership, the team hit major financial problems in 2000 and a fan boycott began in protest over the club's running.[37]

Athletics was another sport where television and sponsor-ship increased its profile and popularity, whilst creating tensions between the amateurist traditions of the administrators and the commercial demands of the stars. After Lynn Davies there were no Welsh athletes of sustained world calibre for twenty years (although Steve Jones did break the world record for the marathon). When Colin Jackson emerged as a world-class hurdler at the end of the 1980s, appearance money, trust funds and sponsorship had transformed athletics. Although Jackson won the world championship in 1993 and 1999, he invariably endured injury or was disappointed when the biggest stage approached. In 1988, he won an Olympic silver but at the 1992, 1996 and 2000 Olympics he finished outside the medals. Jackson, nonetheless, was a world-record holder and in 2002 became the winner of more championship medals than any other British athlete ever. Perhaps Wales's most successful athlete ever is Tanni Grey-Thompson, a spina bifida sufferer from Cardiff who has been confined to a wheelchair since the age of eight. Grey-Thompson won four golds in wheelchair racing at the Barcelona Paralympics (breaking three world records in the process) and another four at the Sydney Paralympics, taking her total haul to thirteen medals in four games. Her other achievements include world championships, world records and marathon golds. Despite her huge sporting achievements and coverage in the celebrity magazine *Hello*, neither Grey nor other disabled athletes fully broke into the lucrative world of sports stardom and they continue to struggle to be treated as equals. Grey-Thompson, herself an important ambassador for disabled sport, remarked that 'No matter how many times you tell them a racing chair is a piece of sporting equipment like Steve Backley's javelin they still respond with the patronising attitude about how brave and wonderful you are.'[38] When she finished third in the BBC's prestigious Sports Personality of the Year in 2000, there was no ramp for her to go on stage to collect her prize.

V

Colin Jackson was born in Cardiff to Jamaican parents who moved to Wales during the large-scale Commonwealth immigration of the 1950s and 1960s. In the wake of this immigration, sport has played a part in promoting racial integration. The popular sporting success of the likes of Jackson, or Olympic hurdler and international rugby cap Nigel Walker, have ensured that not all the symbols of Welsh national identity are white. An apt illustration of the integration that sport can promote is the treatment of Pakistani bowler Waqar Younis. His contribution to Glamorgan's 1997 county championship was celebrated by crowds with chants of 'Waqar is a Welshman'. Yet sport has not always been particularly progressive in its attitudes towards race and it has also demonstrated some of the uglier responses to immigration. Billy Boston was born to West Indian and Irish parents in 1934. Although he had played rugby for Neath and captained the Welsh Boys Clubs, racial attitudes meant that he saw little chance of realizing his ambition of playing cricket for Glamorgan and rugby for Wales. He thus joined Wigan rugby league club, where he became one of the game's finest wingers.[39] Boston was just one of a number of talented black Welsh rugby players who were 'overlooked' in the union game before making their names in rugby league. It was not until 1983 that Mark Brown of Pontypool RFC became the first black player to be capped by Wales at rugby union. On the pitch, black players in both Welsh football and rugby have, on occasions, suffered considerable racist abuse, particularly in amateur and park games. As late as the 1990s, Bobby Gould, the Welsh national soccer manager, was accused of racism by his striker Nathan Blake.[40]

In the 1960s wider controversies over racism spilt over into Welsh sport. In 1961, South Africa was expelled from the Commonwealth because of its apartheid policies but sporting ties continued to exist. In 1964, a Wales rugby team toured South Africa to limited protests from trade unions, churches and other groups. The naïve WRU, despite its disapproval of apartheid, wanted to keep its sport free from political wranglings and maintain sporting contact with one of its traditional opponents. The attitude of most of the players themselves was probably summed up by Barry John, who said that to him, before the 1968 Lions tour to South Africa, apartheid was just 'a vague problem in a hot country far away'.[41] There were far more vocal, and direct, protests against the South African 1969–70 tour of the British Isles, in what was a year of protest across Europe over civil and human rights. The campaign against sporting contact with a racist regime reached violent heights in Swansea, when the pitch was invaded during South Africa's match there. Some of the stewards reacted violently and 200 demonstrators and ten policemen were injured. The next match of the tour, an international at the Arms Park, saw the pitch ringed with barbed wire. 1970 also saw protests over a proposed South African cricket tour of the UK. Wilfred

Wooller of Glamorgan CCC was very vocal in condemning such protests and consequently had his car sprayed with paint. Campaigners dug a four-foot hole in the Sophia Gardens square and sprayed paint on its scoreboard.[42] Eventually, government intervention led to the tour being cancelled. The WRU's continued ambivalent stance on using sport to protest against apartheid caused considerable tensions with a number of Labour-controlled Welsh councils. By the 1980s, many local authorities saw themselves as promoters of and campaigners for social equality. When Zola Budd (a South African who had been given a British passport with almost indecent haste so she could run for Great Britain at the 1984 Olympics) appeared at Cwmbran Stadium, Torfaen District Council protested and tried to display anti-apartheid slogans around the track.[43] But such opposition was ultimately in a minority. As one historian put it, Wales 'seemed to obliterate more profound areas of its moral consciousness in blind pursuit' of sporting entertainment.[44]

Ethnic minorities were not the only group to experience inequalities in Welsh sport. As unemployment rose in the 1970s, there were pockets of significant poverty in Wales. By the early 1980s, the average Welsh household income was approximately 14 per cent below the British average. Inequalities of income naturally impacted on spending on sport. In 1998–9, adult (age fifteen plus) participation in physical activities (including walking two mile plus) was as high as 78.4 per cent in Ceredigion, whereas in deprived Rhondda Cynon Taff it was just 36 per cent. Such inequalities were not simply due to local levels of disposable income. Local authorities have been the most important providers of local sporting facilities. In areas of industrial decline, councils had fewer resources and more important priorities to spend them on. In 1997–8, unsatisfied demand for indoor sports halls in Rhondda Cynon Taff was double the Welsh average, while in Merthyr unsatisfied demand for swimming pools was treble the Welsh average.[45] In all forms of physical recreation, social class has a significant impact on participation levels. In 1998–9, 67 per cent of managers and professionals (social classes AB) participated in physical recreation, while for semi-skilled and unskilled workers (social classes DE) the figure was under 40 per cent.[46] It is in rural Wales where total sports participation is consistently the highest, although when just traditional outdoor sports are considered, then participation rates in the industrial Valleys only fall marginally behind the rest of Wales.[47]

Sport, and rugby in particular, was a masculine world where sexism flourished on the pitch and in the clubhouse. In line with the wider movement for sexual equality, sport did gradually see more openings for women from the 1960s. Yet by 1998–9, while 61.2 per cent of adult men in Wales participated in some form of physical recreation, the figure for women was just 49.1 per cent. For outdoor games, the male participation rate was 24.8 per cent, while for women it was 5.9 per cent.[48] Media attention certainly remained overwhelmingly dominated by male sports, while sportswomen also had to overcome the wider gender problem of balancing a career and parenthood. The loss of form by Kirsty Wade, a triple middle-distance Commonwealth gold medal winner from Llandrindod, reflected such pressures. She noted how becoming a mother stopped her being self-orientated and took away some of her hunger for athletics.[49] Women who played rugby faced the different problem of having their sexuality questioned because of the sport's macho image. Women's rugby began in the UK in universities during the 1970s. In 1983, the Women's Rugby Football Union was established with twelve clubs in England and Wales, and, in 1987, Wales played its first women's international when it took on England at Pontypool. Wales was host to the inaugural women's rugby union world cup in 1991, competed for by twelve teams from whom the USA emerged victorious. Other women's sports in Wales however fell behind progress in England. In 1974, there was just one Welsh club affiliated to the Women's Cricket Association. In contrast, the Swansea Central [male] League alone had four divisions plus two indoors leagues during the 1980s.[50] Barry Ladies FC did win promotion to the women's premier league in 1997, giving female football some profile in Wales. By 2002, there were just over fifty senior women's football clubs in Wales and 400 women and 600 girls registered as players. An indication of the growing acceptance of female sport was the twelve women referees who officiated in men's Welsh football.[51] In women's hockey, Wales even enjoyed some modest success. The outstanding Welsh player of this period was

Anne Ellis MBE, who won 136 consecutive Welsh caps and captained and coached Great Britain Olympic teams. In 1975, the Welsh team finished runners-up in the women's hockey world championship.

Despite an apparent growth in women watching rugby during the 1990s, women's sport in Wales remains far more of a participatory rather than spectator activity. Boosting participation in all sports is part of the remit of the Sports Council for Wales, which was created in 1972 as part of a reorganization of UK sports administration, at a time when Wales's nationhood was increasingly being recognized in public administration. Developing facilities and distributing public money to voluntary sports clubs was another important part of the Sports Council for Wales's role. The setting up of the National Lottery in 1994 also proved a boon to sports facilities in Wales. By June 2002, the Sports Council for Wales had distributed over £68 million of lottery money to over 650 sports projects in Wales. Such funding had a significant impact on the quality and number of sports facilities across Wales. In the 1950s the most popular competitive participatory sport in Wales was said to be bowling.[52] Part of its attraction lay in the fact that older men could participate. By the 1990s, the range of popular sports had diversified into activities that were more about keeping fit than being competitive. Sport was now part of a leisure industry that appealed to people's fears and vanities, as well as their desire for fun and success. Furthermore, the sheer range of sports available was considerable; in 1989, there were 87 different sports governing bodies in Wales.[53]

Figure 1 shows that regular active participation in traditional sports was very much a minority activity, although of course the social function of clubs continued to extend beyond those who actually played. Football may have boasted twice the participation rate of rugby but this did not necessarily measure the difference in the two sport's contributions to local communities.

In the world of outdoor pursuits, Wales enjoys a widespread reputation as a challenging venue. Snowdonia in particular has attracted large numbers of climbers from England, although locals have often been conspicuous by their absence. Wales's popularity for outdoor pursuits has been cemented by the

Figure 1: Top ten sports in Wales by adult
(age 15+) participation, 1998–9[54]

Sport	% of total adults	Sport	% of total adult males	Sport	% of total adult females
Walking	29.3	Walking	28.5	Walking	30.1
Swimming	14.2	Swimming	12.0	Swimming	16.2
Cycling	6.6	Soccer	10.1	Aerobics	5.2
Multigym/ weights	6.3	Cycling	9.4	Multigym/ weights	4.4
Running	5.2	Multigym/ weights	8.4	Cycling	4.0
Soccer	5.1	Snooker	7.8	Dance	3.9
Snooker	4.1	Running	7.6	Running	2.9
Golf	3.7	Golf	6.8	Circuits	1.9
Aerobics	2.9	Rugby	4.3	Badminton	1.3
Dance	2.7	Fishing	3.8	Riding/bowls	1.1

establishment of a number of renowned centres. Plas Menai, on the Menai Straits, was opened in 1983 and is the National Watersports Centre for Wales. Owned by the Sports Council for Wales, it provides facilities for sailing, canoeing, windsurfing, water skiing, rock climbing and mountain leadership and is the only sea-based sports centre in the UK. Capel Curig, in nearby Snowdonia, is the home of Plas y Brenin, the National Mountain Centre which is owned by Sport England. It was opened in 1955 and owes its existence to the creation of the Snowdonia national park in 1948. The establishment of national parks in Snowdonia, the Brecon Beacons and the Pembroke-shire coast has helped develop and preserve the popularity of what the Sports Council for Wales terms the nation's most popular sport, walking. Purists may not define this as a sport at all but it has been important in keeping people healthy and entertained and in opening up the beauty of Wales to a wider audience. Indeed, the sports and activities that the mountains and countryside of Wales offer are among the key attractions highlighted by the marketing of the Wales Tourist Board.

VI

As in so many small nations, sport has offered the people of Wales an important avenue for self-esteem and external recognition. For a nation that exists in the shadow of a powerful cultural and economic neighbour, sport has provided Wales with rare opportunities to celebrate its identity. Thus, as Grand National winning jockeys Hywel Davies and Carl Llewellyn, Badminton Commonwealth gold winner Kelly Morgan, world champion rally driver Gwyndaf Evans or yachtswoman Tracey Edwards have all discovered, the Welsh media has been prone to take a sudden interest in sports otherwise marginal in Welsh culture when there is a Welsh achievement to revel in. In a wider culture that reveres celebrities, stardom could be instant but it could also disappear again as quickly. The culture of celebrity was symptomatic of the changes that sport underwent in the television era. Television caused the profile, diversity and, above all, commercialism of sport to mushroom. The cost was allegedly the exchange of the morals and ethics that made sport great, for the shallowness of money and fame that pervaded a globalized popular culture. Of course, the history of sport suggests that ethics such as playing for the game's sake were never as widespread as was often assumed, but sport has always been interpreted as part of wider readings of society. Whether you agree with the transformation of Glamorgan CCC's Sunday league team into the Glamorgan Dragons, or the placing of company logos on the sacred Welsh rugby jersey, tends to depend on whether you like the general state of popular culture at the end of the twentieth century.

Conclusion

Sport, Wales and the Welsh

In 1999, Wales was the main host for the Rugby World Cup. Although the Welsh team were knocked out in the quarter-finals, four thousand journalists attended the tournament and an estimated three billion viewers watched on television. At the heart of the tournament was the state-of-the-art Millennium Stadium, purpose-built with lottery money on the site of the Cardiff Arms Park. Characteristic of contemporary Welsh politics, the stadium's genesis and construction had been controversial. But, despite doubts over the wisdom of knocking down the thirty-year-old national stadium and concerns over whether a replacement could be built in time, the hopes instilled in the stadium stretched far beyond providing Welsh rugby with a modern new home. Barcelona's hosting of the Olympics had been central to its successful regeneration and led other European cities to view sport as a means of encouraging economic development. As part of a wider regeneration strategy, Cardiff had already unsuccessfully bid to host the 1986 Commonwealth games. The local authority in Cardiff was integral to the process of securing the necessary lottery funding for the Millennium Stadium, which it saw as having the possibility to become 'the engine house of prosperity for the next 50 years, attracting investment and tens of thousands of visitors to Cardiff and Wales, helping regenerate large areas of the heart of the Welsh capital'. Thus it was envisaged that the stadium would be a symbol of hope, progress and pride for Cardiff and Wales.[1] Implicit in this vision was the modernity of the project. The marketing of the stadium made clear that it was one of the finest stadiums in the world, whilst, in its retractable roof, the stadium boasted a feature that was hi-tech, progressive and (in Europe) unique. Indeed, the stadium's very name (which was disliked by traditionalists within rugby) suggested something for the future. Thus it was hoped that the stadium would be more than just a contributor to the economic well-being of Cardiff and Wales; it was to be a symbol of what sort of places they were, or at least wanted to be.

However, the actual impact on Cardiff and Wales of the stadium and the Rugby World Cup was not as clear-cut as first predicted. Only eight of the forty-one matches were actually held in Wales. The rest were held in the other home nations and France and thus many visitors got their first and only sight of Wales on the day of the final. Meanwhile, Welsh fans who were not members of rugby clubs found it difficult to obtain tickets. City-centre traders complained that their takings were severely down on match days and even the media coverage was mixed and limited in its coverage of non-sporting Wales. Indeed, there is no firm evidence that increased media coverage actually attracts investment in any case.[2] Furthermore, doubts remain about the stadium's long-term ability to attract the frequency of use it needs to be economically viable. Nonetheless, both the World Cup and stadium clearly contributed to a 'feel good factor' in the city and increased the profile of Cardiff and Wales on the international sporting stage. Residents are proud both of the building and the events that it has hosted. In its short life, the Millennium Stadium has become something of a Welsh icon. It even became the temporary home of that most English of institutions, the FA Cup final, to much acclaim in England and amidst contrasting negative publicity over the future of Wembley stadium.

The marketing video for the world cup – a mixture of castles, beautiful scenery and the guitar-thrashing Manic Street Preachers – attempted to relate the so-called national sport with wider images of a modern vibrant Wales that enjoys a rich heritage. This may be a select view of Wales past and present but there does exist a relationship between sport and Welsh national identity that stretches back into the late nineteenth century. Quantifying the exact nature of this relationship is an impossible task, made more difficult by the shifting and plural nature of Welsh identity. 'Wales is an artefact which the Welsh produce', wrote historian Gwyn A. Williams, 'the Welsh make and remake Wales day by day and year by year'.[3] Exactly what that artefact is, is a contentious question obscured by current political ideas about Wales's future, the absence of a nation state and prominent internal geographic, linguistic and ethnic divisions. Wales as a unified entity is thus an 'imagined community'[4] and Welshness has a plethora of different meanings for the people who possess and make it. However one defines Wales, it would be difficult to deny sport's place in the inventing, maintaining and projecting of the idea of a Welsh national identity within and outside Wales's blurred borders, even if the Wales that sport has projected has varied according to time, place and context.[5] Although the Welsh language, music and Nonconformity have also played their part, few other cultural forms are as well equipped as sport to express national identity. Its emotions, national colours, emblems, songs and contests all make it a perfect vehicle through which collective ideas of nationhood can be expressed. Rugby internationals, for example, have mobilized Wales's collective identities and passions. They gloss over the different meanings that the people of Wales attach to their nationality, enabling them to assert their Welshness in the face of internal division and the political, social and cultural shadow of England. As Eric Hobsbawm put it, 'the imagined community of millions seems more real as a team of eleven [or fifteen] named people'.[6]

Tanni Grey-Thompson remarked 'I've had so much support being a Welsh athlete, which has made it very important to me. I'm very proud of being a Welsh athlete'.[7] Yet to sporting audiences, the national pride associated with individual sports has never been as prominent, vocal or festive as that seen in team sports. The fandom associated with sports such as athletics is arguably more passive and less communal and outwardly emotional than that associated with rugby or football. Individual sports certainly attract fewer supporters than team sports. Furthermore, the symbolism of an individual pursuit is perhaps less immediately conducive to the construction of group consciousness. In rugby or football, the players are competing for a team named after or clearly associated with a given geographical place, and this collective identity, which the notion of the team inspires, takes precedence over the individual identities of team members. For example, English players in a Welsh club football team collectively become representatives of Wales. Even racist football fans seem able to accept black players in their team because an individual's skin colour is seen as secondary to the wider collective club identity. In individual sports, even where an athlete is competing for a national team, this is not entirely possible. The athlete retains his or her identity as an individual. Indeed, modern media coverage of sport plays up their individual traits and quirks.[8] This makes it difficult for the individual to appeal to all the different communities and prejudices that make up a nation. A further complication is that where individuals do officially represent a nation at a sport, it is as likely to be Great Britain as it is Wales. Colin Jackson, for example, might represent Wales at the Commonwealth Games but he more often races as a British athlete, and particularly so on the prestigious Olympic stage. None of this is to argue that individual sportsmen and women have not become symbols of Welsh nationhood, but it does suggest that, in sport, it is teams rather than individuals that are the most potent and accessible symbols of Wales.

Of course, not everyone likes sport. The events where sport reaches a much wider audience than normal (for example, the alleged 100,000 who took to the streets to welcome home Cardiff City's FA Cup winners in 1927) are few and far between. The 1999 Wales versus England rugby international at Wembley attracted 600,000 television viewers in Wales. Although this did not include people watching in pubs and clubs and was a significantly higher proportion of the viewing audience than in England, it still only represents around one in five people in Wales.[9] In the 1997 Welsh Referendum Study, only 49 per cent of the representative sample claimed to be very proud of the Welsh rugby team.[10] Neither rugby nor sport are quite the dominant Welsh obsession that many would like to believe and this limits the role sport can play in projecting and forging national identity. In the Edwardian period, sport played an important role in incorporating English in-migrants into a Welsh national identity that was being reconstructed in order to maintain its distinctiveness and inclusiveness in the face of mass in-migration from an economically and politically dominant neighbour. But other ethnic minorities in Wales have also been the subject of continuous racial prejudice and marginalization. Rugby and football have continually attracted female support but the sports have always been male dominated and have even at times deliberately excluded women. David Andrews has argued that the new Welsh national identity of the late Victorian and Edwardian periods was very much a male construct, which ignored women and reinforced the patriarchal nature of society. The role of rugby in promoting this identity was particularly illustrative of this male domination.[11] Female support and involvement in traditionally male sports may have increased in the late twentieth century but women remain marginal within the culture of those sports and thus the national identity that they project. Furthermore, as sexual discrimination increasingly became socially unacceptable, sport could even act as something of a last bastion of traditional ideas of male domination and gender roles. After Wales had beaten England in 1993, a Welsh rugby correspondent at *The Observer* wrote, 'Once it has sunk in today, the singing in the chapels will be heavenly and afterwards the pubs will be joyfully overflowing and the Welsh womenfolk will be baking their Welsh cakes and taking their men to their bosoms.'[12] This may be tongue-in-cheek journalism but at another level such rhetoric illustrates and perhaps perpetuates the male chauvinism that still dominates popular perceptions of what Welshness is and of where sport fits into that Welshness. Nonetheless, one does not have to be liberated by or actively interested or involved in sport to be aware of its existence and proclamations of nationhood. As media coverage of sport, and indeed the actual audience of the popular media, grew in the post-1945 period, it became far harder for people to be unaware or untouched by sport. Many women may not have not felt directly included in the process but extensive media coverage ensured that sport maintained and developed its role as an agent in projecting national identity.[13]

Richard Holt has argued that cultural identity is a two-way process.[14] Sport has not only helped the Welsh see themselves as a nation, it has also helped others accept Welsh nationhood. Wales may not have a presence on the international political stage but it does have a long history of its own national teams and associations, many of which have attracted considerable media attention. These institutions formed an integral part of the limited civil Welsh society that existed over the course of the twentieth century. Furthermore, they have enjoyed a more popular relevance than the host of quangos and other national bodies that grew up after the administrative devolution of the 1960s and beyond. On both sides of the border, the media coverage of such teams may have indulged in national clichès and stereotypes, but the media is nonetheless important in constructing and transmitting popular discourses and ideas of nationhood.[15] The relationship with England is crucial to an understanding of Welsh identity. Linda Colley has written, 'men and women decide who they are by reference to who and what they are not. Once confronted with an obviously alien "Them", an otherwise diverse community can become a re-assuring or merely desperate "Us".'[16] Thus one of the agencies that has driven the Welsh to make and remake Wales is a sense of being different from England. This may derive from some sense of a common inheritance or even, at times, alleged racial Celtic qualities, but these are vague and, arguably, mythical qualities that are certainly not inclusive in a nation with a rich history of immigration. What sport has done, more tangibly and inclusively, is to bring alive a sense of 'otherness' and difference in the relationship between Wales and England that would otherwise be almost invisible and often alienating to so-called 'incomers'.

How Wales responds to that 'other' has varied across sports, place and time. There is little evidence of any active tension between the Welsh and English immigrants in the south Wales coalfield before the Second World War.[17] Probably thanks in part to such movements of people, sporting contests against England in this period seem to have been imbued with friendly rivalry rather than the passionate anti-English antagonism found in England-Scotland football matches. The growth of anti-Englishness in Welsh sport seems to date from the 1960s, when wider Welsh nationalism took on the more overt, confident and even confrontational character noted in chapter four. Today, the healthy state and prominent television coverage of Welsh club rugby (at least in comparison with Welsh soccer) mean that very few people in Wales support an English rugby club and thus there is little individual identification between Welsh fans and English players. Welsh rugby sees itself on a par with England. Even where there are not current successes to match such rhetoric, there are shared memories of victories from the past. Thus the English national XV takes on the persona of the arrogant neighbour who must and can be cut down to size. This persona is further developed by English rugby's middle-class and establishment associations, which contrast unfavourably with the more populist image of rugby in Wales. Arguably, few Welsh rugby fans would support England against non-British sides, let alone other 'Celtic' nations. Yet there has been widespread support for a British league because of its potential to develop Welsh players more fully than a Welsh league. Anti-Englishness is not, then, incompatible with an appreciation of Britain.

Welsh football in contrast has always operated firmly within an English context. The rise of a more aggressive and younger fan culture in the later 1960s coincided with the growth of a more assertive national consciousness. Since this period, Welsh club football has become loaded with provocative national emotions when teams meet English rivals. By the 1970s chants at Cardiff City included 'Supertaffs' and 'Bloody English, all illegitimate . . . Bastards every one'.[18] It is now commonplace for players and referees who commit fouls or give dubious decisions at Welsh grounds to be greeted with choruses of 'You cheating English bastard'. Away fans are taunted with the name of whichever team has last beaten England. Any attempt to respond is likely to be drowned out by 'England's full of shit', to the tune of the English football anthem, *Three Lions*. Yet the Premiership's prolific marketing and branding, together with its domination of televised football, mean that the English national team is full of familiar faces who play for teams with strong followings in Wales. Manchester United and Liverpool shirts are even common sights on the home terraces of Swansea and Wrexham. There is substantial anecdotal evidence to suggest that when England has played important games in recent World Cups or European Championships, it has tended to find substantial numbers of supporters in the pubs and living rooms of Wales. With the Welsh national XI not remotely on a par with England, fans could support the old enemy without feeling they were compromising their Welsh identity. There were, of course, substantial numbers of soccer fans who supported whoever

England was playing, especially amongst the ranks of supporters of Wales's three Football League clubs, but understandings of what being Welsh required have always differed. Even amongst such fans (as well as supporters of the three semi-professional teams who play in English non-league football), there has been strong opposition to their joining the League of Wales. Such a move would bring about a decline in standards and financial insecurity: sporting standards and financial needs are clearly viewed as more important than any notion of standing independently on one's own feet. Indeed, to fans of Cardiff City, Swansea City and Wrexham, playing in an English rather than a Welsh league, with all its opportunities to taunt and beat the English 'other', is actually a way of declaring one's Welshness. Although modern Welsh football demonstrates the complexity and perhaps contradictions of Welsh identity, it also needs to be judged within the context of a football culture that celebrates and even creates rivalries, hatreds and divides.[19] Even the aggressive assertions of fans (such as 'Being a Welsh football fan makes me hate the English with a passion'[20]) have to be taken a pinch of salt, fun and bravado. Other sports certainly do not feature such an aggressive anti-Englishness. In short, there is no single monolithic Welsh identity.

Despite its plurality, the more oppositional pride in Welshness has been driven forward by the wider process of globalization. A corollary of a global media and economy pushing towards a homogenized western culture has been a resurgence of interest in local traditions, customs and identities. This has the purpose of consciously highlighting the alleged unique features of a domestic culture that might not, at first, seem particularly different from those elsewhere in the world. As well as promoting Wales's difference, sport also signalled Wales's place in this wider global culture. In addition to the Welsh rugby and Premiership shirts one can see on the streets of any Welsh town or city, there are also American baseball caps and training tops bearing global brand names such as Nike and Reebok. Sport in Wales is part of a wider leisure industry that is geared around looking good. By 1998, annual expenditure on sport in Wales was £585.89 million, which represented 2.52 per cent of the nation's total consumer expenditure.[21] It is this overt commercialism that is the most significant difference between sport's current cultural form and its roots in the late nineteenth and early twentieth centuries.

In 1997, Robert Croft, the England and Glamorgan cricket bowler, said that when he and his fellow players turned out for Glamorgan they were representing Wales, while being chosen to play for England in a test match was like being picked for the British Lions.[22] Welsh sport has consistently required fans and players to make such rationalizations about their national identity, even if only subconsciously. The pride players have declared on being picked for the British Lions also perhaps suggests a pride in Britishness that extends beyond the achievement of being honoured at one's profession. Sport has certainly signalled Wales's Britishness in a variety of fashions. Welsh athletes compete for Great Britain at the Olympics, while Welsh fans cheer on English, Scottish and Northern Irish athletes running and jumping for the Union Jack. It is perhaps symptomatic of the nature of popular Welsh identity that the sports, such as rugby, which came to embody Welshness, were imported from England, while the traditional Welsh games discussed in chapter one fell away. Yet, even the games and customs of traditional Welsh rural culture had little to distinguish them from their equivalent in England.[23] Indeed, the whole chronology and character of sport in Wales has closely followed its equivalent in England. There were of course minor variations in the form Welsh sport took but even here there was little that was truly unique. Welsh rugby's working-class following may have contrasted with rugby's middle-class base in the south of England but it was replicated in northern England, allowing for the division into league and union. Nor was the game as democratic as many contemporaries, and some historians, liked to believe.[24] Administrative control of rugby remained firmly in the hands of the professional and industrial middle class that took it from the public schools to the workers. Even more recent 'distinct' elements of Welsh rugby, such as hymn singing and the waving of mascots such as giant leeks, have their direct parallels in other sports' fan cultures. Finally, rugby's alleged domination over football in Wales is certainly not true of the north and debatable in the south, both in terms of players and followers.

As Neil Evans has argued, Wales is more clearly an idea than a society.[25] Once we begin to strip away the gloss of what makes

Wales different, we actually discover that social structure is as much a defining element of Welsh society as national identity. Sport crossed the boundaries of class but it also reinforced them. The gentry might patronize the traditional communal pastimes of rural Wales but they also indulged in activities such as hunting that were concerned with emphasizing social status. Similarly, from the late nineteenth century until at least the 1960s, support for team sport crossed the social cleavages of class but grounds were divided along the contours of wealth between the stands and terraces. Other sports were characterized by the needs and values of those who played them. Golf, for example, was a sport riven by snobbery and a middle-class desire to distance itself from the masses. In contrast, the world of local football and rugby was based upon neighbourhood and working-class community institutions such as pubs and welfare halls, while the games themselves were played in the physical and competitive spirit of working-class life. Even after the 1960s, as class divisions became more fluid and less overt, sport continued to act as a signifier of social status and aspirations, with participation rates varying significantly according to class and gender. Thus, while on the one hand sport projected the idea of a national Welsh community, on the other it was shaped by the social divisions of everyday life.

Even discourses of what united and constituted the Welsh nation are contested. Despite sport's role in promoting Welsh identity, in the late nineteenth and early twentieth centuries, it was resented by elements of the Welsh-speaking middle class because it signalled Wales's place in a wider British and working-class culture. In 1885, *Y Faner* called rugby a 'bestial sport' and its popularity 'indisputable proof that this "Age of Light" is returning to the "Land of Darkness"'.[26] The cultural nationalism that sport represented was clearly distinct from the national consciousness promoted by Nonconformity, Liberalism and especially *Eisteddfodau* and the associated Welsh-language culture. Middle-class visions of the Welsh *gwerin*, that mythical, religious, classless and respectable rural Welsh-speaking people, did not include crude and commercial entertainments. On the whole the Welsh-language press largely ignored sport until at least the 1890s.[27] Even in 1907 one writer could ask 'who would turn to a Welsh paper for an account of the Derby, or the Oxford and Cambridge boat race?'[28] After the First World War, as sport clearly gained respectability in the eyes of other bastions of Welsh-language culture, such as Nonconformity or even the Urdd (a Welsh-language youth movement), the intellectual Welsh-language press remained aloof in its attitudes towards sport. While the English-language Welsh media celebrated the 1927 FA Cup final as a national achievement, the Welsh-language press overlooked it or treated it as an English event.[29] Such attitudes were shaped by wider fears for the future of the language and all it meant. Sports such as soccer and rugby were strongest in industrial Wales, where the decline of the language was most evident. Sport was one symbol of the new mass culture that was replacing the old respectable culture associated with speaking Welsh.

Yet sport did have a place in the culture of Welsh-speaking people, rather than in Welsh-speaking culture. R. Merfyn Jones's study of quarrymen in Gwynedd in the late nineteenth and early twentieth centuries depicts a people immersed in a Welsh-language culture of prose and poetry. But Jones also shows that, alongside the *eisteddfodau*, sports such as football and billiards had their popular place in the lives of these Welsh speakers. Sport's place in the culture of Welsh-speaking people was often partly through the medium of English. *Yr Udgorn*, a Welsh-language paper in north-west Wales, reported on football matches in English. Sport's rules and terminologies thus introduced new English words into the vocabulary of Welsh speakers.[30] Even in the inter-war years, sports still had English names amongst Welsh-speaking children in rural west Wales.[31] It was not until the 1950s that the FAW became the first national sports association to translate its rules into Welsh. The first book on sport to be published in Welsh did not appear until 1958.[32] In the Welsh-speaking village in north Pembrokeshire where I grew up in the late 1970s and 1980s, 'football' (never *pêl-droed*) was probably the integral element of our free time, self-esteem and relationships with our peers. Not until Swansea City's successes of the early 1980s was there a Welsh club to rival to the loyalties that Manchester United and Liverpool found in this relatively isolated corner of *Cymru Gymraeg* (Welsh-speaking Wales). Because sport was so embedded in the fabric of life in Welsh-speaking Wales, an opposition to sport was not sustainable if mainstream Welsh-language culture wished to become more populist. A poem about a rugby international who abandoned sport for a life as a missionary had symbolically but controversially won the crown at the National Eisteddfod in Bangor in 1931.[33] The pragmatic adoption of sport was evident in the increasingly sympathetic attitude of the nationalist party, Plaid Cymru, to sport. In the inter-war years, Saunders Lewis, the leader of Plaid Cymru, looked upon industrial Wales and its culture as symptomatic of a nation that had become morally and economically degenerate. Yet by the late 1980s the party was using images of Commonwealth-gold winner Colin Jackson, wrapped in a Welsh flag, in one of its election broadcasts. By 1995, the party could even be found indulging in sentimental nonsense about a natural link between sport and the Welsh: 'Welsh people have rugby in their blood; they are born to play and they are born to win'.[34]

Given Plaid Cymru's consistent lack of success in parliamentary elections outside its Welsh-speaking heartland, it might be suggested that Wales has largely been a nation of eighty- and ninety-minute patriots: people who are willing to cheer their Welshness for the length of a game but then meekly accept the safety of existing within Britain.[35] At the end of a decade when pride and success in Welsh rugby had probably been at its highest, only 11.8 per cent of the electorate (and 20.3 cent of the turnout) voted in favour of the creation of a Welsh assembly at the 1979 devolution referendum. K. O. Morgan noted that

> Welsh identity, so easily asserted in pounding the Saxon on the rugby field, was too easily diverted, in the view of more serious nationalists, from the quest for national independence. Rugby and investitures, the bread and circuses of the populace, became a peaceful therapy to suppress embarrassing political aspirations . . . most of the Welsh were content to have it that way. They rejoiced in their rugby skills, made no protest, and asked few questions.[36]

Sport may have been patriotism enough for some but there is little to suggest that it actually minimized political nationalism in Wales on any significant basis. Identities are contextual and situational: taking pride in one's nation on the rugby field is one thing, taking a leap into the dark of political autonomy is quite another. This is not a contradiction or a sign of some limitation in Welshness but simply economic pragmatism and evidence of the complex plurality of Welsh identity.

In 1992, the Campaign for a Welsh Assembly declared, 'Welsh rugby, once a source of national pride, has now become part of that rapid erosion of identity which has thrown a big question-mark over what it means to be Welsh today'.[37] The decline in Welsh rugby fortunes after the 1970s may have lessened one traditional source of Welsh pride but more fundamental to any wider crisis of identity was the decline of the traditional Welsh industries and the rule of a Conservative government whose support across Wales was limited. The social and political alienation brought about by the Conservative governments of 1979–97 was arguably key in raising support for devolution and sharpened people's sense that Wales had distinct political needs from England.[38] The election of the first Labour government for eighteen years coincided with what seemed to be a new patriotic confidence in Wales, as the character of Welsh identity shifted again. The success of a number of Welsh rock bands was perhaps the most obvious manifestation of what the media christened 'Cool Cymru', and a song by Catatonia declared to the world 'Every day when I wake up I thank the Lord I'm Welsh'.[39] By 1999, even BBC Wales felt bold enough to run a television trailer for its rugby coverage that centered on Kelly Jones of the Stereophonics singing 'as long as we beat the English we don't care'. When Wales did beat England with a last gasp try in 1999 a *Western Mail* editorial extolled, 'Confidence is a wonderful state of mind. The Welsh team now has it in abundance and, more importantly, it has rubbed off on the rest of the nation. It's a day to be proud'.[40] Much of this trumpeted pride in Wales had a lighthearted feel. In 1998, the *Western Mail* made dramatic front-page associations between a rugby clash against England and the rebellion of Owain Glyndŵr.[41] Yet, for all the paper's pride in Wales, its editorial line remains firmly one that is committed to a devolved Wales within a wider British state. Despite this cultural confidence in Wales, the 'Yes' vote at the 1997 devolution referendum was won by only 6,721 votes in a 50.3 per cent turnout. The use of popular Welsh sports stars and

other celebrities to mobilize a 'Yes' vote had evidently not been
entirely successful.[42] The 1997 Referendum Survey suggested
that Welsh people are very divided in how they see their
national identity, with only 17 per cent denying that they had
any British identity.

Figure 2: Self-description of national identity by
respondents in 1997 Referendum Survey[43]

	%
Welsh, not British	17
More Welsh than British	26
Equally Welsh and British	34
More British than Welsh	10
British, not Welsh	12

Furthermore, 23 per cent of the sample who saw themselves as
Welsh not British still voted 'No' in the referendum.[44] In
contrast to Scotland, popular doubts remain about whether
devolution has had any positive benefits for Wales. The nation
might have its own Assembly, not to mention a world-class
stadium, but it has remained committed to the British state
and a British culture within which it can take pride in its
multiple identities.

Thus sport illustrates and contributes to the complexity of
Welsh identity. Despite the enthusiasm with which many
people throughout the twentieth century have voiced their
patriotism, Wales also exists within a British culture, and
increasingly, a global culture. What the idea of Wales means is
as divided as the nation itself: 'Wales as a nation is one
organizing principle, but so is Wales as a collection of disparate
regions.'[45] Sport, too, has given voice to these local and
regional identities, from the era of parish games to the modern-
day commercialized club scene. Indeed, the simplistic notion
of a north-south split in the devotions to rugby and football is
a basic but vivid indicator of a divided nation. The historical
experience of the people of south Wales has certainly been
much closer to the other industrial regions of Britain than it

has to rural west and north Wales. The post-war influence of television has as much brought rural Wales further into a wider British popular culture as it has cemented the idea of unified Wales. Like all nations, Wales is divided by the basic structures of region, ethnicity, class and gender and this has shaped its sporting culture.

Yet, whichever Wales people belong to, sport has offered them something more relevant that just a sense of nationhood. For many men in industrial Wales, sport offered a shared experience that helped them come to terms with urban life. Along with the pubs, chapels, and working-men's institutes, it was often one of the key social institutions. The culture of sport was shaped by the values of this wider community. It was competitive, hard and macho; it offered a physical satisfaction that manual labour did not. This was the male working class making, or at least shaping, its own culture, rather than simply accepting and absorbing the cultural forms and values handed down to it by the middle classes. This industrial sporting culture also shared common properties with the sporting culture of other parts of Wales. Rural sport, be it the village football club or the local tug-of-war team, was equally imbued with notions of local patriotism, heroism and sociability. Even in middle-class sports, the historian can see sport's role in providing companionship and status for a group, men and women, that was geographically dispersed and lacked the sociability of neighbourhood life.

Such experiences are recurring themes in the history of sport. Across the last two hundred years people have drawn pleasure from watching and playing physical games. The exact form of these games has obviously changed with the contexts in which they took place but common characteristics remain. Winning has always been important to people, both for themselves as individuals and for their wider community. People have enjoyed betting on the outcome of these contests. Some have seen sport as a way of making money; others have remained opposed to such 'tainting' of a cultural form that was supposed to teach 'higher' values. In all these properties, there is nothing at all unique about Welsh sport. It is thus much safer to talk of sport in Wales than Welsh sport. And yet the most popular sports in Wales are caught up with the idea of Wales. They were a collective experience that helped sustain a popular and collective Welsh national identity that crossed the cleavages of class and region. Women may have often been excluded from this experience but this was typical of many aspects of public life, popular culture and the national identity that sport both helped sustain and project. Merfyn Jones has argued that the Welsh are increasingly becoming defined 'not in terms of shared occupational experience or common religious inheritance or the survival of an ancient European language or for contributing to the Welsh radical tradition, but rather by reference to the institutions that they inhabit, influence and react to'.[46] The creation of the National Assembly for Wales signals another redefinition of Wales based upon an institution that has the potential to bestow an inclusive citizenship on people. Sport may thus become less important in defining how the Welsh see themselves and how others see them. Yet debate continues about whether de-volution has gone too far or not far enough. As the intensity of such arguments increases, sport will probably continue to offer a rare refuge where many of the Welsh people can unite, if only temporarily.

Notes

Chapter 1

1. George Owen, (Henry Owen, ed.), *The Description of Pembrokeshire* [1603] (London, 1892) pp. 270–82.

2. *Bye-Gones Relating to Wales and the Border Counties*, vol. 8, 2 March 1887, p. 264. The important account of folk football in this source was based on the writer's conversations with 'aged people in two or three Cardiganshire towns'.

3. *Bye-Gones Relating to Wales and the Border Counties*, vol. 8, 2 March 1887, p. 263.

4. Richard Suggett, 'Festivals and social structure in early modern Wales', *Past and Present*, 152 (August 1996), 79–112.

5. D. G. Lloyd, *Pwllheli: An Old Welsh Town and its History* (Pencader, 1991), ch. 8.

6. Emma Lile, 'Athletic Competition in Pre-Industrial Wales' (MPhil thesis, University of Birmingham, 1994), p. 36.

7. Edmund Hyde Hall (ed. E. G. Jones), *A description of Caernarvonshire in 1809–11* (Caernarfon, 1952), p. 318.

8. Prys Morgan, 'From a death to a view: The hunt for the Welsh past in the Romantic Period', in Eric Hobsbawm and Terence Ranger (eds), *The Invention of Tradition* (Cambridge, 1983), p. 54.

9. Gareth Williams, *1905 and all that: Essays on Rugby Football, Sport and Welsh Society* (Llandysul, 1991), p. 114.

10. Charles Redwood, *The Vale of Glamorgan: Scenes and Tales among the Welsh* (London, 1839), pp. 173–9.

11. Emma Lile, 'Professional pedestrianism in south Wales during the nineteenth century', *The Sports Historian*, 20, 2 (November 2000), 94–105.

12. Translation from Gareth Williams, 'Postponing death: sport and literature in Wales', *New Welsh Review*, 36 (Spring 1997), 40.

[13] A. H. Dodd (ed.), *A History of Wrexham* (Wrexham, 1957), pp. 239, 241.

[14] Williams, *1905 and all that*, p. 118.

[15] Harriet Ritvo, *The Animal Estate: The English and Other Creatures in the Victorian Age* (London, 1987), ch. 3.

[16] *Bye-gones relating to Wales the Border Counties*, vol. 8, 1886–7, p. 264. Religious attacks on traditional pastimes have a long history in Wales. Dancing and games, for example, were condemned in cleric satirist Ellis Wynne's *Gweledigaetheu y Bardd Cwsc* (Visions of the Sleeping Bard) (Cardiff, [1704], 1948).

[17] Suggett, 'Festivals and social structure', p. 88.

[18] Suggett, 'Festivals and social structure', p. 87. For an example of a festival in Angelsey lasting until 1899 see O. Hughes, *Hanes Plwyf Trefdraeth* (Bangor, *c*.1905), pp. 77–80.

[19] Neil Evans, '"As rich as California. . ." Opening and closing the frontier: Wales, 1780–1870', in Gareth Elwyn Jones and Dai Smith (eds), *The People of Wales* (Llandysul, 1999), p. 118.

[20] Hall, *Description of Caernarvonshire*, p. 321.

[21] Edward Jones, *The Bardic Museum,* 1802, quoted in Prys Morgan, 'From a death to a view', p. 44.

[22] Quoted in Hilarie M. Waddington, 'Games and athletics in bygone Wales', *Transactions of the Honourable Society of Cymmrodorion* (1953), p. 97.

[23] See Waddington, 'Games and athletics', p. 95.

[24] Prys Morgan, 'From a death to a view', pp. 54–5.

[25] *Gentleman's Magazine*, 1839, p. 599, quoted in Waddington, 'Games and athletics', p. 93.

[26] Quoted in Lile, 'Professional pedestrianism', p. 94.

[27] Quoted in Williams, *1905 and all that*, p. 125.

[28] Williams, 'Postponing death', p. 40.

[29] There is a large literature debating the survival/disappearance of traditional forms of popular culture in the early nineteenth century. For a summary see Neil Tranter, *Sport, Economy and Society in Britain, 1750–1914* (Cambridge, 1998), ch. 2.

[30] For example: '[He] had been a wild youngster and a noted player, but having been lately converted at a Methodist Revival, had not been without some difficulty persuaded to take a part in this match.' Redwood, *Vale of Glamorgan*, p. 177.

31 *The Red Dragon*, vol. 6, September 1884, p. 284. This quote has been erroneously attributed to Neath in some previous work.

32 William Plomer (ed.), *Kilvert's Diary, 1870–1879* (Harmondsworth, 1977 edn), p. 159.

33 *The Cambrian*, 6 June 1851, quoted in Lile, 'Athletic competition in pre-industrial Wales', appendix.

34 R. J. Moore-Colyer, 'Field Sports, conservation and the countryside in Georgian and Victorian Wales', *Welsh History Review*, 16, 3 (1993), p. 315; D. J. V. Jones, 'The poacher: a study in Victorian crime and protest', *Historical Journal*, 22, 4 (1977), 825–60; Russell Davies, *Secret Sins: Sex, Violence and Society in Carmarthenshire, 1870–1920* (Cardiff, 1996), pp. 128–31.

35 *The Field, The Country Gentleman's Newspaper*, 24 April 1897, p. 617.

36 David Jones has similarly argued that there were two concepts of justice and order, the official and the popular. David Jones, *Crime in Nineteenth Century Wales* (Cardiff, 1992).

37 Moore-Colyer, 'Field sports', p. 316.

38 Linda Colley, *Britons: Forging the Nation, 1707–1837* (London, 1994 edn), pp. 170–2.

39 Capt. Leach, Pembrokeshire, 1870 quoted in David W. Howell, 'Leisure and recreation, 1815–1974', in David W. Howell (ed.), *Pembrokeshire County History: vol. IV, Modern Pembrokeshire, 1815–1974* (Pembrokeshire, 1993), p. 419.

40 Moore-Colyer, 'Field sports', p. 321.

41 Leslie Baker-Jones, *Princelings, Privilege and Power: The Tivyside Gentry in their Community* (Llandysul, 1999), p. 185.

42 Quoted in Moore-Colyer, 'Field sports', p. 322.

43 Quoted in Derek Birley, *Sport and the Making of Britain* (Manchester, 1993), p. 325.

44 R. J. Moore-Colyer, 'Gentlemen, horses and the turf in nineteenth-century Wales, *Welsh History Review*, 16, 1 (1992). Quote from p. 52.

45 Quoted in Dodd, *History of Wrexham*, p. 242.

46 Martin Johnes, 'Archery, romance and elite culture in England and Wales, *c*.1780–1840', *History*, 89, 2 (2004), 193–208.

47 Royal British Bowmen minutes, quoted in Col. H. Walrond, 'Some old archery societies', in C. Longman and Col. H. Walrond, *Archery* (London, 1894), ch. 12; Gwilym Usher, 'The Society of Royal British Bowmen (1787)', *Denbighshire Historical Society Transactions*, 4 (1955), 85–90.

48   Plomer, *Kilvert's Diary*, p. 157.
49   Plomer, *Kilvert's Diary*, p. 60.
50   Andrew Hignell, *A 'Favourit' Game: Cricket in South Wales before 1914* (Cardiff, 1992).
51   Hignell, *'Favourit' Game*, p. 72.
52   Hignell, *'Favourit' Game*, p. 28.
53   *Monmouthshire Merlin*, 1843, quoted in Hignell, *'Favourit' Game*, p. 40.
54   Birley, *Sport and the Making of Britain*, p. 254.
55   Hignell, *'Favourit' Game*, p. 61.
56   Quoted in Hignell, *'Favourit' Game*, p. 38.
57   J. A. Mangan, *Athleticism in the Victorian and Edwardian Public School* (Cambridge, 1981).
58   Quoted in John Harris, 'The birth and development of football in Breconshire', *One Day in Leicester: The Second Journal of the Association of Sports Historians* (Chislehurst, 1996), p. 38.
59   W. J. Townsend Collins (ed.), *Newport Athletic Club: The Record of Half a Century* (Newport, 1925), p. 10.
60   *Brecon Journal*, 28 March 1861, cited in Harris, 'birth and development of football in Breconshire', p. 37.
61   Quoted in David Smith and Gareth Williams, *Fields of Praise: The Official History of the Welsh Rugby Union, 1881–1981* (Cardiff, 1980), p. 24.
62   Collins, *Newport Athletic Club*, pp. 12–20.
63   Smith and Williams, *Fields of Praise*, p. 10.
64   Smith and Williams, *Fields of Praise*, p. 55.
65   Collins, *Newport Athletic Club*, p. 14.
66   Red Dragon, 'Reminiscences of the Cardiff Rugby Football Club', in CRFC, *Opening Ceremony of the New Stands, Cardiff Arms Park, Souvenir Programme*, 5 October 1910.
67   *The Pembrokeshire Herald*, quoted in Howell, 'Leisure and recreation', p. 429.
68   A. Howkins, 'The discovery of rural England', in Robert Colls and Philip Dodd (eds), *Englishness, Politics and Culture, 1880–1920* (Beckenham, 1986); Georgina Boyes, *The Imagined Village: Culture, Ideology and the English Folk Revival* (Manchester, 1993); Morgan, 'From death to a view'.
69   Suggett, 'Festivals and social structure', p. 88.
70   Owen, *Description of Pembrokeshire*.
71   *Bye-gones relating to Wales and the Border Countries*, vol. 6, 19 April 1899.

72 Taff Ely Rod Fishing Association minutes (1890s), Glamorgan Record Office: D/D TE/1/1.

73 Collins, *Newport Athletic Club*, pp. 146–7.

74 H. J. Jones, *Nelson Handball Court: History of the Court and its Players, 1860–1940* (Nelson, nd). Kevin Dicks, 'Welsh handball', in Richard Cox, Grant Jarvie and Wray Vamplew, *Encyclopedia of British Sport* (Oxford, 2000), p. 416.

75 *Merthyr Express*, 3 July 1880, cited in Andrew J. Croll, 'Civilizing the urban: popular culture, public space and urban meaning, Merthyr *c*.1870–1914' (Ph.D., University of Wales, 1997), ch. 4.

Chapter 2

1 Quoted in David Smith and Gareth Williams, *Fields of Praise: The Official History of the Welsh Rugby Union, 1881–1981* (Cardiff, 1980) p. 57. The account of rugby presented here owes much to this book.

2 Chris Williams, *Capitalism, Community and Conflict: The South Wales Coalfield, 1898–1947* (Cardiff, 1998), p. 69.

3 A. J. Gould quoted in Smith and Williams, *Fields of Praise*, p. 84.

4 W. J. Townsend Collins (ed.), *Newport Athletic Club: The Record of Half a Century* (Newport, 1925), p. 38.

5 Quoted in Smith and Williams, *Fields of Praise*, p. 5.

6 *The Pembrokeshire Herald*, 22 April 1887, quoted in David W. Howell, 'Leisure and Recreation, 1815–1974', in David W. Howell (ed.), *Pembrokeshire County History: vol. IV, Modern Pembrokeshire, 1815–1974* (Pembrokeshire, 1993), p. 418.

7 Smith and Williams, *Fields of Praise*, pp. 12, 86, 102–3; Gareth Williams, *1905 and all that: Essays on Rugby Football, Sport and Welsh Society*, (Llandysul, 1991), p. 18.

8 Collins, *Newport Athletic Club*, p. 48.

9 Smith and Williams, *Fields of Praise*, p. 125; Williams, *1905 and all that*, pp. 145–51.

10 Tony Collins, *Rugby's Great Split: Class, Culture and the Origins of Rugby Football League* (London, 1998).

11 *Llanelly Mercury* quoted in Derek Birley, *Land of Sport and Glory: Sport and British Society, 1887–1910* (Manchester, 1995), p. 49.

A History of Sport in Wales

[12] Smith and Williams, *Fields of Praise*, pp. 77, 119.

[13] Quotes from *South Wales Graphic*, 18 October 1902 and from letter by secretary of Halifax Cricket and Football Club in *South Wales Graphic*, 6 December 1902.

[14] WFU executive member speaking of the Rhondda in 1901. Quoted in Williams, *1905 and all that*, p. 155.

[15] Williams, *1905 and all that*, pp. 159–66; Peter Lush and Dave Farrar (eds), *Tries in the Valleys: A History of Rugby League in Wales* (London, 1998).

[16] *Western Mail*, 3 October 1910.

[17] Quoted in Smith and Williams, *Fields of Praise*, p. 101.

[18] Quoted in Williams, *1905 and all that*, p. 77.

[19] *South Wales Daily News*, 18 December 1905.

[20] Smith and Williams, *Fields of Praise*, ch. 7 looks at this game in detail.

[21] For claims for such a connection see A. G. Bradley, *Highways and Byways in South Wales* (London, [1903] 1931), p. 319.

[22] Quotes from Williams, *1905 and all that*, p. 78.

[23] Arthur Gould in C. B. Fry's Magazine, October 1906. Quoted in Brian Dobbs, *Edwardians at Play: Sport 1890–1914* (London, 1973), pp. 100–1. Italics in original.

[24] David Parry Jones, *Prince Gwyn: Gwyn Nicholls and the First Golden Era of Welsh Rugby* (Bridgend, 1999).

[25] Dai Smith, *Wales: A Question for History* (Bridgend, 1999), p. 118.

[26] Occupations derived from Gareth M. Davies and Ian Garland, *Who's Who of Welsh International Soccer Players* (Wrexham, 1991).

[27] Ian Garland, *The History of the Welsh Cup, 1877–1993* (Wrexham, 1993). Martin Johnes and Ian Garland, '"The new craze": football and society in north-east Wales. *c*.1870–90', *Welsh History Review*, 22, 2 (2004), 278–304.

[28] John Harding, *Football Wizard: The Story of Billy Meredith* (Derby, 1985).

[29] Martin Johnes, *Soccer and Society: South Wales, 1900–39* (Cardiff, 2002), ch. 1 and conclusion.

[30] *The Times*, 18 March 1889.

[31] Nevill Miroy, *The History of Hockey* (Lakeham-on-Thames, 1986), pp. 172–9; *South Wales Graphic*, 22 November 1902; Collins, *Newport Athletic Club*, pp. 186–92.

[32] *South Wales Graphic*, 6 September 1902.

[33] Claire Parker, 'The rise of competitive swimming, 1840 to 1878', *The Sports Historian*, 21, 2 (2001), 54–67.

34 Ian Keil and Don Wix, *In the Swim: The Amateur Swimming Association from 1869 to 1994* (Loughborough, 1996), p. 245.

35 Albert Baker, *The History of Quoits in Wales: International and Individual Records* (Abertillery, 1949).

36 For similar arguments relating to Scotland see Neil Tranter, 'Quoiting' in Grant Jarvie and John Burnett (eds), *Sport, Scotland and the Scots* (Phantassie, 2000).

37 John Lowerson, *Sport and the English Middle Class, 1870–1914* (Manchester, 1995), p. 50.

38 Quoted in Leslie Baker-Jones, *Princelings, Privilege and Power: The Tivyside Gentry in their Community* (Llandysul, 1999), p. 188.

39 Quoted in Mark Robinson and Peter Less, *Golf Courses of North Wales* (Wilmslow, 1997), p. v.

40 Raymond J. Stroud, 'The landscape of popular recreation in Newport, Monmouthshire, 1888–1914' (MA thesis, University of Wales, 1993), p. 146.

41 D. G. Lloyd, *Pwllheli: An Old Welsh Town and its History* (Pencader, 1991), ch. 8.

42 C. M. Traver, *Penarth Yacht Club: A Centenary History* (Published by club, 1980), pp. 26, 27; Penarth Yacht Club minutes, Special General Meeting, 10 March 1894. Glamorgan Record Office: DYPC/1.

43 For a wider view of the social panic created by cycling see Geoffrey Pearson, *Hooligan: A History of Respectable Fears* (London, 1983), pp. 66–9. For cycling in general see David Rubinstein, 'Cycling in the 1890s', *Victorian Studies*, 21, 1 (1977), 47–72.

44 Simon Craig, 'Riding high', *History Today*, 50, 7 (July 2000), 18–19.

45 W. J. Edwards, *From the Valley I Came* (London, 1956), pp. 21–5.

46 Andrew J. Croll, 'Civilizing the urban: popular culture, public space and urban meaning: Merthyr *c*.1870–1914' (Ph.D., University of Wales, 1997), ch. 4.

47 Stan Shipley, 'Boxing', in Tony Mason (ed.), *Sport in Britain: A Social History* (Cambridge, 1989), pp. 87–8.

48 Welsh boxers and their relationship with society are explored in Dai Smith 'Focal heroes: a Welsh fighting class', in Richard Holt (ed.), *Sport and the Working Class in Modern Britain* (Manchester, 1990).

49 Andrew Horrall, *Popular Culture in London, c.1890–1918: The Transformation of Entertainment* (Manchester, 2001), pp. 126, 139–40, 204.

50　Smith, 'Focal heroes'.

51　R. Merfyn Jones, 'The mountaineering of Wales, 1880–1925', *Welsh History Review*, 19, 1 (June 1998), 44–67.

52　Hignell, *'Favourit' Game*, especially pp. 123, 128, 179. Also see his *The History of Glamorgan CCC* (London, 1988).

53　Jack Williams, 'Cricket', in Tony Mason (ed.), *Sport in Britain: A Social History* (Cambridge, 1989), p. 127.

54　Emma Lile, 'Women and sport in Aberystwyth, 1870–1914' (MA thesis, University of Wales, 1995), pp. 14, 31, 56; Traver, *Penarth Yacht Club*, p. 8; Brian Lile and David Farmer 'The early development of association football in south Wales, 1890–1906', *Transactions of the Honourable Society of Cymmrodorion* (1984), p. 203.

55　For an account of Wales and the First World War see Angela Gaffney, *Aftermath: Remembering the Great War in Wales* (Cardiff, 1998), ch. 1.

56　*South Wales Daily News*, 3 September 1914.

57　Quoted in Williams, *1905 and all that*, p. 27.

58　Johnes, *Soccer and Society*, pp. 109–12.

59　Hignell, *'Favourit' Game*, p. 133; Peter Foley, *Gaelic Athletic Association: Gloucestershire County Board A Brief History from 1949–1999* (Gloucestershire, 2000); Johnes, *Soccer and Society*, p. 97.

60　Linda Colley, *Britons: Forging the Nation, 1707–1837* (London, 1994 edn), p. 6.

Chapter 3

1　For inter-war soccer in south Wales see Martin Johnes, *Soccer and Society: South Wales, 1900–39* (Cardiff, 2002).

2　Martin Johnes, 'Fred Keenor', in Peter Stead and Huw Richards (eds), *For Club and Country: Welsh Football Greats* (Cardiff, 2000), pp. 33–44.

3　On inter-war rugby I have relied heavily on David Smith and Gareth Williams, *Fields of Praise: The Official History of the Welsh Rugby Union, 1881–1981* (Cardiff, 1980).

4　Gareth Williams, 'The road to Wigan Pier revisited: the migration of Welsh rugby talent since 1918', in John Bale and Joseph Maguire (eds), *The Global Sports Arena: Athletic Migration in an Interdependent World* (London, 1994), p. 26.

Also see Robert Gate, *Gone North: Welshmen in Rugby League*, vols. 1 and 2 (Ripponden, 1986 and 1988).

5   David Boucher, *Steel, Skill and Survival: Rugby in Ebbw Vale and the Valleys, vol. 1, 1870–1952* (Ebbw Vale, 2000), pp. 114–18.

6   Sullivan quoted in Williams, 'The road to Wigan Pier', p. 25.

7   Colin Baber and Dennis Thomas, 'The Glamorgan economy, 1914–45', in Arthur H. John and Glanmor Williams (eds), *Glamorgan County History, vol. V: Industrial Glamorgan* (Cardiff, 1980); Gareth Williams, *1905 and all that: Essays on Rugby Football, Sport and Welsh Society*, (Llandysul, 1991), pp. 178–79.

8   Phil Melling, *Man of Amman: The Life of Dai Davies* (Llandysul, 1994).

9   Peter Lush and David Farrar (eds), *Tries in the Valleys: A History of Rugby League in Wales* (London, 1998).

10   Ystrad Mynach Golf Club, minutes of general meeting of ladies' section, 9 December 1932, Glamorgan Record Office: D/DX 519, 1, 2.

11   Glyn Eden, *Ffestiniog Golf History: The First Hundred Years* (Published by the club, 1992), pp. 14–15.

12   A. J. Lush, *The Young Adult in South Wales* (Cardiff, 1941), pp. 76–7; Rhys Davies, *My Wales* (London, 1937), p. 108.

13   Small stake gambler quoted in Philip Massey, 'Portrait of a mining town', *Fact*, 8 (November 1937), p. 53; *South Wales Echo*, 8 December 1928; Mark Clapson, *A Bit of a Flutter: Popular Gambling and English Society, c.1823–1961* (Manchester, 1992) offers a wider history of betting in Britain.

14   Brain Lee, *The Great Welsh Sprint: The Story of the Welsh Powderhall Handicap, 1903–34* (Pontypridd, 1999), quote from p. 54.

15   Jack Williams, 'Cricket', in Tony Mason (ed.), *Sport in Britain: A Social History* (Cambridge, 1989), pp. 127, 137.

16   Andrew Hignell, *A Who's Who of Glamorgan County Cricket Club* (Derby, 1992) and *Maurice Turnbull: A Welsh Sporting Hero* (Stroud, 2001).

17   Andrew Hignell, *The Skipper: a Biography of Wilf Wooller* (Litlington, 1995).

18   *South Wales Echo* and *South Wales Football Echo*, 14 March 1936.

19   Smith and Williams, *Fields of Praise*, p. 223.

20   Williams, *1905 and all that*, p. 187; Gordon West, *A Century on the Beat: A History of 100 Years of Police Rugby Football in the South Wales Constabulary Area* (Cardiff, 1992); Smith and Williams, *Fields of Praise*, p. 223.

21   Quoted in Williams, *1905 and all that*, p. 194.
22   Bernard Darwin, *British Sport and Games* (London, 1940), p. 25.
23   Quoted in Smith and Williams, *Fields of Praise*, p. 283.
24   Mike Huggins, *Racing and British Culture 1918–1939* (Manchester, 2003), ch. 5.
25   Quoted in Smith and Williams, *Fields of Praise*, p. 231.
26   Johnes, *Soccer and Society*, ch. 6.
27   K. L. Little, *Negroes in Britain: A Study of Racial Relations in English Society* (London, 1947), pp. 42, 51, 140; Johnes, *Soccer and Society*, pp. 96, 126; Paul Thompson, *The Edwardians: The Remaking of British Society* (London, 1992), p. 100.
28   Mari A. Williams, ''In the wars': Wales, 1914–45', in Gareth Elwyn Jones and Dai Smith (eds), *The People of Wales* (Llandysul, 1999), p. 189.
29   For a brief account of the early history of sport on the radio see Raymond Boyle and Richard Haynes, *Power Play: Sport, The Media and Popular Culture* (Harlow, 2000), pp. 33–8.
30   A. J. P. Taylor, *English History, 1914–45* (Oxford, 1965), p. 313.
31   Lynn Hughes, *Pendine Races: Motor Racing over Fifty Years* (Llandysul, 2000).
32   Jack Jones, *Rhondda Roundabout* (London, 1934) p. 8.
33   Norman Baker, 'Going to the dogs – hostility to greyhound racing in Britain: Puritanism, socialism and pragmatism' *Journal of Sport History*, 23, 2 (Summer 1996), p. 103.
34   Walter Haydn Davies, *Blithe Ones* (Bridgend, 1979), p. 90.
35   *Western Mail*, 5 April 1928.
36   Huggins, *Racing and British Culture*, ch. 5.
37   Bob Lonkhurst, *Man of Courage: The Life and Career of Tommy Farr* (Lewes, 1997), p. 10.
38   This analysis of Farr is based upon Dai Smith, 'Focal heroes: a Welsh fighting class', in Richard Holt (ed.), *Sport and the Working Class in Modern Britain* (Manchester, 1990).
39   Stephen Ridgwell, 'South Wales cinema in the 1930s', *Welsh History Review*, 17, 4 (1995), p. 608.
40   Martin Johnes, 'Pigeon racing and working-class culture in Britain, c.1870–1950', *Cultural and Social History*, forthcoming
41   Martin Johnes, 'Poor man's cricket: baseball, class and community in south Wales, c.1880–1950', *International Journal of the History of Sport*, 17, 4 (2000), 153–66.

42 E. J. Thomas, 'The history of physical education in Wales to 1970' (M.Ed. thesis, University of Manchester, 1979), p. 162.

43 *Confectioners' Union*, 1925 quoted in Ian Pincombe, 'Out of Rexville: G. F. Lovell and the south Wales confectionery industry, c. 1830–c. 1940' (Ph.D. thesis, University of Wales, 2000), p. 243.

44 R. Emlyn Jones, *Llandyrnog and District Village Clubs' Summer Football League: The Official History, 1927–1995* (Published by Llandyrnog and District Village Clubs' Summer Football League, 1995).

45 Quoted in C. M. Traver, *Penarth Yacht Club: A Centenary History* (Published by club, 1980), p. 28.

46 St Fagan's Lawn Tennis Club minutes, 1925–35, Museum of Welsh Life, 3770/1–2.

47 Smith and Williams, *Fields of Praise*, p. 122.

48 Welsh Schools Football Association, *Official Handbook*, 1933–4.

49 E. Colston Williams, 'Physical culture in Wales', *Welsh Outlook*, 6 (1919), p. 309.

50 For more on street and school football see Johnes, *Soccer and Society*, ch. 3.

51 Smith and Williams, *Fields of Praise*, p. 301.

52 Attendances from Brian Tabner, *Through the Turnstiles* (Harefield, 1992).

53 David Parry-Jones, 'Sport for all and the new riches', in David Cole (ed.), *The New Wales* (Cardiff, 1990), p. 163.

54 Grahame Lloyd, *C'mon City: A Hundred Years of the Bluebirds* (Bridgend, 1999), p. 140.

55 John Charles, *King of Soccer* (London, 1957), p. 149.

56 Mario Risoli, *When Pelé Broke our Hearts: Wales and the 1958 World Cup* (Cardiff, 1998).

57 Smith and Williams, *Fields of Praise*, p. 340.

58 Trefor M. Owen, 'Chapel and community in Glan-Llyn, Merioneth', in David Jenkins, Emrys Jones, T. Jones Hughes and Trefor M. Owen, *Welsh Rural Communities* (Cardiff, 1960), p. 233.

59 Alwyn D. Rees, *Life in a Welsh Countryside: A Social Study of Llanfihangel yng Ngwynfa* (Cardiff, 1971), p. 140.

60 Ronald Frankenberg, *Village on the Border: A Social Study of Religion, Politics and Football in a North Wales Community* (London, 1957), quotes from 100, 102.

[61]   Wyn Williams (ed.), *Sport in Wales* (Denbigh, 1958), p. 73.

[62]   Brian Lee, *Cardiff Voices* (Stroud, 2000), p. 127.

[63]   *The Official History of the VIth British Empire & Commonwealth Games, 1958 – Cardiff/Wales* (Published by the organising committee, 1958).

Chapter 4

[1]   Richard Holt and Tony Mason, *Sport in Britain, 1945–2000* (Oxford, 2000), p. 47.

[2]   See Bill Samuel, *Rugby: Body and Soul* (Edinburgh, 1998).

[3]   J. P. R. Williams, *JPR: The Autobiography of J. P. R. Williams* (London, 1979), p. 15.

[4]   John Davies, *A History of Wales* (Harmondsworth, 1993), p. 644.

[5]   Lyrics to the best of Boyce's work can be found at his website: www.maxboyce.co.uk

[6]   Idris Davies, *Gwalia Deserta*, part XXXIII, 1938, Islwyn Jenkins (ed.), *The Collected Poems of Idris Davies* (Llandysul, 1980 edn), p. 46.

[7]   Emrys Jones (ed.), *The Welsh in London* (Cardiff, 2001).

[8]   Williams, *JPR*, p. 19; Barry John, *The Barry John Story* (London, 1973).

[9]   John, *Barry John Story*, p. 53.

[10]   Joseph Maguire and Jason Tuck, 'Global sports and patriot games: rugby union and national identity in a United sporting Kingdom since 1945', in Mike Cronin and David Mayall (eds), *Sporting Nationalisms: Identity, Ethnicity, Immigration and Assimilation* (London, 1998), pp. 103–126.

[11]   Davies, *History of Wales*, p. 644.

[12]   John, *Barry John Story*, pp. 13–14.

[13]   Richard Holt, *Sport and the British: A Modern History* (Oxford, 1989), p. 253.

[14]   Quoted in Martin Polley, *Moving the Goalposts: A History of Sport and Society Since 1945* (London, 1998), p. 60.

[15]   David Smith and Gareth Williams, *Fields of Praise: The Official History of the Welsh Rugby Union, 1881–1981* (Cardiff, 1980) p. 375.

[16]   K. O. Morgan, *Rebirth of a Nation: Wales, 1880–1980* (Cardiff/ Oxford, 1981), pp. 134, 348.

[17]   For Welsh rugby in the 1980s and 1990s see Dai Smith and Gareth Williams, 'Beyond the fields of praise: Welsh rugby,

1980–1999', in Huw Richards, Peter Stead and Gareth Williams (eds), *More Heart and Soul: The Character of Welsh Rugby* (Cardiff, 1999), pp. 205–32.

18 Holt and Mason, *Sport in Britain*, p. 50; Smith and Williams, 'Beyond the fields of praise', pp. 219–20.

19 Jonathan Davies with Peter Corrigan, *Jonathan: An Autobiography* (London, 1990).

20 Quoted in Adrian Smith, 'Civil war in England: the clubs, the RFU, and the impact of professionalism on rugby union, 1995–99', in Adrian Smith and Dilwyn Porter (eds), *Amateurs and Professionals in Post-War British Sport* (London, 2000), p. 150.

21 Gareth Davies (Cardiff RFC) quoted in Siân Nicholas, 'Gareth Davies', in Richards et al., *More Heart and Soul*, p. 157.

22 Rob Hughes, 'John Charles' in Peter Stead and Huw Richards, *For Club and Country: Welsh Football Greats* (Cardiff, 2000), 99–109.

23 Grahame Lloyd, *C'mon City: A Hundred Years of the Bluebirds* (Bridgend, 1999), p. 174.

24 *Western Mail*, 1 August 1966.

25 Manchester United, *http://www.manutd.com/supporters/ brancheswales.sps* (accessed 9 October 2001).

26 *When Saturday Comes*, 187 (September 2002), p. 46.

27 Martin Johnes, 'Hooligans and barrackers: crowd disorder and soccer in south Wales, 1906–39', *Soccer and Society*, 1, 2 (2000), 19–35.

28 BBC Sport, *http://news.bbc.co.uk/sport/hi/english/other_sports/newsid_1291000/1291283.stm* (accessed 18 December 2001).

29 The only other time this feat has been achieved anywhere in the world in first class cricket was in 1984–5 by Ravi Shastri for Bombay.

30 *Western Mail*, 5 August 1964.

31 Grahame Lloyd, *Daffodil Days: Glamorgan's Glorious Summer* (Llandysul, 1998).

32 Holt, *Sport and the British*, p. 319.

33 Leighton Rees with Dave Lanning, *Leighton Rees on Darts* (London, 1979), quote from p. 4.

34 Ray Physick and Richard Holt, '"Big money": the tournament player and the PGA, 1945–75', in Smith and Porter (eds), *Amateurs and Professional*, pp. 60–80.

35 BBC Sport. *http://newssearch.bbc.co.uk/sport/hi/english/wales/newsid_1704000/1704174.stm* (accessed 13 December 2001).

36   Sports Council for Wales, *Golf in Wales*, Sports Update 38 (March 1999).

37   Andrew Weltch, *Images of Sport: Cardiff Devils* (Stroud, 2001); Anthony Beer, *It's Funny When You Win Everything: The Story of the Cardiff Devils, 1986–1994* (Abergavenny, 1994).

38   Quoted in Holt and Mason, *Sport in Britain*, p. 16.

39   Phil Melling, 'Billy Boston', in Huw Richards, Peter Stead and Gareth Williams (eds) *Heart and Soul: The Character of Welsh Rugby* (Cardiff, 1998), pp. 47–58; Robert Gate, *Gone North: Welshmen in Rugby League, vol. 1* (Ripponden, 1986), pp. 108–20.

40   Neil Evans and Paul O'Leary, 'Playing the game: sport and ethnic minorities in modern Wales', in Neil Evans, Paul O'Leary and Charlotte Williams (eds), *A Tolerant Nation? Exploring Ethnic Diversity in Wales* (Cardiff, 2003); Mark Burley and Scott Flemming, 'Racism and regionalism in Welsh soccer', *European Physical Education Review*, 3, 2 (1997), 183–94. For a wider discussion of sport and ethnicity see Polley, *Moving the Goalposts*, ch. 6.

41   John, *Barry John Story*, p. 87.

42   Jack Williams, *Cricket and Race* (Oxford, 2001), p. 71; Andrew Hignell, *The Skipper: a Biography of Wilf Wooller* (Litlington, 1995).

43   Jeremy Crump, 'Athletics', in Tony Mason (ed.), *Sport in Britain: A Social History* (Cambridge, 1989), p. 76.

44   Morgan, *Rebirth of a Nation*, p. 349.

45   Sports Council for Wales (SCW), *Sport and Rural Wales*, Sports Update 43 (February 2001).

46   SCW, *Sports Participation and Club Membership in Wales 1998/99*, Sports Update 44 (February 2001), p. 12.

47   Adult participation in outdoor games: Metropolitan Wales 14.2 per cent; Rural Heartland 17.2 per cent; The Valleys 13.1 per cent; Rural North 18.1 per cent, SCW, *Sports Participation and Club Membership in Wales 1998/99*, p. 6.

48   SCW, Sports Participation and Club Membership in Wales 1998/99, p. 8.

49   Ellis Cashmore, *Sports Culture: An A-Z Guide* (London, 2000), p. 281.

50   Jack Williams, 'Cricket', in Mason, *Sport in Britain*, pp. 141, 127.

51   Information from Alun Evans, Football Association of Wales, June 2002.

52 Bill Jones, 'Bowls', in Wyn Williams (ed.), *Sport in Wales* (Denbigh, 1958), p. 73.

53 David Parry-Jones, 'Sport for all and the new riches', in David Cole (ed.), *The New Wales* (Cardiff, 1990), p. 166.

54 SCW, *Sports Participation and Club Membership in Wales 1998/99*, pp. 9–10.

Conclusion

1 Russell Goodway, Cardiff County Council leader quoted in *Western Mail Survey*, 15 May 1996.

2 See Calvin Jones, 'Mega events and host region impacts: determining the true worth of the 1999 rugby world cup', *International Journal of Tourism & Hospitality Research*, 3, 3 (2001), 241–51.

3 Gwyn A. Williams, *The Welsh in their History* (London, 1982), p. 200.

4 Benedict Anderson, *Imagined Communities: Reflections on the Origins and Spread of Nationalism* (London, 1983).

5 For similar arguments in relation to Scotland see Grant Jarvie and Irene A. Reid, 'Sport, nationalism and culture in Scotland', *The Sports Historian*, 19, 1 (November, 1999), 97–124.

6 Eric Hobsbawm, *Nations and Nationalism since 1780* (Cambridge, 1990), p. 143.

7 Quoted at HTV Wales Sport, *http://www.htvwales.com/sport/* (accessed 9 October 2001).

8 This emphasis on personality in the television coverage of sport is part of a wider soap opera-like presentation of sport. See Raymond Boyle and Richard Haynes, *Power Play: Sport, the Media and Popular Culture* (Harlow, 2000), pp. 189–91.

9 Communication with BBC Information Wales, 8 July 2002.

10 Although the survey identified rugby as second to the landscape in prompted 'sources of national pride', the response was only 3 per cent higher than for male voice choirs. John Curtice, 'Is Scotland a nation and Wales not?' in Bridget Taylor and Katarina Thomson (eds), *Scotland and Wales: Nations Again?* (Cardiff, 1999), p. 127.

11 David Andrews, 'Sport and the masculine hegemony of the modern nation: Welsh rugby, culture and society, 1890–1914', in John Nauright and Timothy J. Chandler (eds), *Making Men: Rugby and Masculine Identity* (London, 1996), pp. 50–69.

[12] Quoted in Joe Maguire, 'Sport, identity politics, and globalization: diminishing contrasts and increasing varieties', *Sociology of Sport Journal*, 11, 4 (1994), p. 412.

[13] Such ideas are briefly developed in Garry Whannel, 'Individual stars and collective identities in media sport', in Maurice Roche (ed.), *Sport, Popular Culture and Identity* (Brighton, 1998), pp. 34–5.

[14] Richard Holt, *Sport and the British: A Modern History* (Oxford, 1989), p. 237.

[15] See Boyle and Haynes, *Power Play*, ch. 8.

[16] Linda Colley, *Britons: Forging the Nation, 1707–1837* (London, 1992), p. 6.

[17] Chris Williams, *Capitalism, Community and Conflict: The South Wales Coalfield*, 1898–1947 (Cardiff, 1998), p. 70.

[18] Paul Harrison, 'Soccer's tribal wars [1974]', in Paul Barker, *The Other Britain: A New Society Collection* (London, 1982), p. 246.

[19] Gary Armstrong and Richard Giulianotti (eds), *Fear and Loathing in World Football* (Oxford, 2001).

[20] Cardiff City fan in Dougie and Eddy Brimson, *England, My England: the Trouble with the National Football Team* (London, 1996), p. 192. Occasionally, anti-English chanting throws up debates on fan websites about whether it constitutes some form of racism. The dominant opinion seems to be that such behaviour should be regarded light-heartedly.

[21] Consumer expenditure on sport included travel, gambling, sports footware and subscription to sports television channels. Sport also provided 20,542 jobs in Wales in 1998. This represented 1.78 per cent of total employment in Wales that year. Figures from Sports Council for Wales, *Economic Impact of Sport in Wales, 1998* (SPORTfact no. 3, November 2000).

[22] Quoted in *The Times*, 29 December 1997.

[23] A point made in Richard Suggett, 'Festivals and social structure in early modern Wales', *Past and Present*, 152 (August 1996), p. 112.

[24] For a misreading of Welsh rugby see Eric Dunning and Kenneth Sheard, *Barbarians, Gentlemen and Players: A Sociological Study of the Development of Rugby Football* (Oxford, 1979).

[25] Neil Evans, 'Writing the social history of modern Wales: approaches, achievements and problems', *Social History*, 17, 3 (1992), p. 485.

[26] Quoted in Dai Smith, *Wales: A Question for History* (Bridgend, 1999), p. 71.

27 Aled Jones, *Press, Politics and Society: A History of Journalism in Wales* (Cardiff, 1993), p. 52.

28 W. Eilir Evans, 'Newspapers and Magazines of Wales', in T. Stephens (ed.), *Wales To-day and To-morrow* (Cardiff, 1907), p. 347.

29 Martin Johnes, *Soccer and Society: South Wales, 1900–39* (Cardiff, 2002) pp. 205–6.

30 D. G. Lloyd, *Pwllheli: An Old Welsh Town and its History* (Pencader, 1991), ch. 8.

31 Conversations between the author and former pupils at Ysgol Gynradd Hermon, Pembrokeshire.

32 Howard Lloyd (ed.), *Crysau Cochion: Cymry ar y Maes Chwarae* (Llandybie, 1958); E. J. Thomas, 'The history of physical education in Wales to 1970' (M.Ed. thesis, University of Manchester, 1979), p. 246.

33 David Smith and Gareth Williams, *Fields of Praise: The Official History of the Welsh Rugby Union, 1881–1981* (Cardiff, 1980), p. 271.

34 Laura McAllister, 'The Welsh sporting dilemma', *Agenda* (Summer 1997), p. 45; quote from *http://www.bbc.co.uk/dna/h2g2/A580303* (accessed 22 July 2002).

35 After the 1992 general election, Jim Sillars of the Scottish National Party famously complained that 'Scotland has too many ninety minute patriots whose nationalist outpourings are expressed only at major sporting events.' Quoted in Grant Jarvie and Graham Walker (eds), *Scottish Sport in the Making of the Nation: Ninety Minute Patriots* (Leicester, 1994), p. 1.

36 K. O. Morgan, *Rebirth of a Nation: Wales, 1880–1980* (Cardiff/Oxford, 1981), p. 134.

37 Quoted in Meic Stephens, *Wales in Quotation* (Cardiff, 1999), p. 128.

38 For a brief account of the changing political climate in Wales, 1979–99 see J. Barry Jones and Denis Balsom (eds), *The Road to the National Assembly for Wales* (Cardiff, 2000), chs, 1 and 2 and Kevin Morgan and Geoff Mungham, *Redesigning Democracy: The Making of the Welsh Assembly* (Bridgend, 2000), part one. For changing attitudes in Wales also see Geoffrey Evans, 'Why was 1997 different?', in Bridget Taylor and Katarina Thomson (eds), *Scotland and Wales: Nations Again?* (Cardiff, 1999), pp. 95–117.

39 Chorus to title track on Catatonia's *International Velvet* album (Blanco Y Negro, 1998).

[40] Quoted in Stephens, *Wales in Quotation*, p. 135.

[41] *Western Mail*, 21 February 1998.

[42] Leighton Andrews, 'Too important to be left to the politicians: the 'Yes' for Wales story', in Jones and Balsom, *The Road to the National Assembly*, pp. 50–69. The 'No' campaign also tried to use celebrities, with footballer Gary Speed countering Ryan Giggs's support for a 'Yes' vote. David McCrone and Bethan Lewis, 'The Scottish and Welsh referendum campaigns', in Taylor and Thomson, *Scotland and Wales*, p. 32.

[43] John Curtice, 'Is Scotland a nation and Wales not?', in Taylor and Thomson, *Scotland and Wales*, p. 125.

[44] Ibid., p. 129.

[45] Martin Daunton, Review of K. O. Morgan's *Rebirth of Nation*, in *English Historical Review*, XCVII, (January 1982), p. 161.

[46] R. Merfyn Jones, 'Beyond identity? The reconstruction of the Welsh', *Journal of British Studies*, 31 (1992), p. 356.

Further Reading

My sources for specific information in the book can be found in the endnotes. For those who wish to explore the social history of sport in Wales further, this section outlines the key sources. Attention is also drawn to wider British or English studies of sports that were prominent in Wales.

For rugby I have drawn extensively on the work of Dai Smith and Gareth Williams. Their co-authored *Fields of Praise: The Official History of the Welsh Rugby Union, 1881–1981* (Cardiff, 1980) is a tour de force of sports history that combines a deep understanding of the game with a perceptive analysis of its relationship with wider society. Some of the themes from this book are further developed in Williams's collection, *1905 and all that: Essays on Rugby Football, Sport and Welsh Society*, (Llandysul, 1991) and his essay on the migration of Welsh players to rugby league, 'The road to Wigan Pier revisited: the migration of Welsh rugby talent since 1918', in John Bale and Joseph Maguire (eds), *The Global Sports Arena: Athletic Migration in an Interdependent World* (London, 1994). For a slightly different slant on Welsh rugby see David Andrews, 'Sport and the masculine hegemony of the modern nation: Welsh rugby, culture and society, 1890–1914', in John Nauright and Timothy J. L. Chandler (eds), *Making Men: Rugby and Masculine Identity* (London, 1996), which explores how rugby's relationship with Welsh national identity illus-trated the patriachical nature of that identity. For rugby post-1980 see Dai Smith and Gareth Williams, 'Beyond the Fields of Praise: Welsh rugby, 1980–1999', in Huw Richards, Peter Stead and Gareth Williams (eds), *More Heart and Soul: The Character of Welsh Rugby* (Cardiff, 1999), which continues the style and

rigour of their earlier book. Useful populist histories of Welsh
rugby include Alun Richards, *A Touch of Glory: 100 years of
Welsh Rugby* (London, 1980). Max Boyce, *I was There* (London,
1979) captures the flavour of the heady days of the 1970s.

Autobiographies in all sports tend to reveal little about their
subjects. The most useful products of the Welsh game are
probably J. P. R. Williams, *JPR: The Autobiography of J. P. R.
Williams* (London, 1979); Jonathan Davies (with Peter Corrigan),
Jonathan: An Autobiography (London, 189) and Barry John, *The
Barry John Story* (London, 1973). Bill Samuel, *Rugby: Body and
Soul* (Edinburgh, 1998) is an evocative account of a school-
teacher's relationship with rugby and Gareth Edwards in
particular. It is also key to anyone wishing to understand the
place of rugby in the culture, and particularly the education
system, of south Wales. For biographies of Welsh players, often
considering what the players meant to the writers, see Huw
Richards, Peter Stead and Gareth Williams (eds), *Heart and
Soul: The Character of Welsh Rugby* (Cardiff, 1998), and its
sequel, Huw Richards, Peter Stead and Gareth Williams (eds),
More Heart and Soul: The Character of Welsh Rugby (Cardiff,
1999). There is little social history on rugby in specific places,
although David Boucher, *Steel, Skill and Survival: Rugby in Ebbw
Vale and the Valleys, 1870–1952* (Ebbw Vale, 2000) is a notable
exception. Club histories tend to be too celebratory and prone
to descending into bland match descriptions. David Farmer,
The Life and Times of Swansea RFC: The All Whites (Swansea,
1995), however, is something of an exception. For rugby
league in Wales, Peter Lush and Dave Farrar (eds), *Tries in the
Valleys: A History of Rugby League in Wales* (London, 1998) is a
useful but somewhat disjointed collection. Robert Gate, *Gone
North: Welshmen in Rugby League*, vols 1 and 2 (Ripponden,
1986 and 1988) looks at the careers of Welshmen who went
north. Phil Melling, *Man of Amman: The Life of Dai Davies*
(Llandysul, 1994) is an entertaining and perceptive biography
of a lesser-known Welsh league player. Tony Collins, *Rugby's
Great Split: Class, Culture and the Origins of Rugby Football League*
(London, 1998) is an excellent social history of rugby league.
There is little academic work on rugby history in general,
although Gareth Williams does contribute an overview of the
union game in Tony Mason (ed.), *Sport in Britain: A Social*

History (Cambridge, 1989), an essay reproduced in revised form in his *1905 and all that*. Sean Smith, *The Union Game: A Rugby History* (London, 1999) is a selective but useful contribution to the game's history. Further sources on rugby and Wales can be traced via the exhaustive John Jenkins, *A Rugby Compendium: An Authoritative Guide to the Literature of Rugby Union Football* (London, 1998).

For academic work on Welsh football, Martin Johnes, *Soccer and Society: South Wales, 1900–39* (Cardiff, 2002) is a detailed account of the international, club and local game. The account of hooliganism is developed in Martin Johnes, 'Hooligans and barrackers: crowd disorder and soccer in south Wales, 1906–39', *Soccer and Society*, 1, 2 (2000), 19–35. For the early history of the game see Brian Lile and David Farmer 'The early development of association football in south Wales, 1890–1906', *Transactions of the Honourable Society of Cymmrodorion* (1984), 193–215, and for a beginning on the post-war game see Martin Johnes, 'Irredeemably English? Football as a Welsh sport', *Planet: The Welsh Internationalist*, 133 (February-March 1999), 72–9. On north Wales see Martin Johnes and Ian Garland, '"The new craze": football and society in north-east Wales, *c.*1870–1890', *Welsh History Review*, 22, 2 (2004), 278–304. For a specific club within its community see Martin Johnes, 'Mushrooms, scandal and bankruptcy: the short life of Mid Rhondda FC', *The Local Historian*, 32, 1 (2002), 41–53. Ronald Frankenberg, *Village on the Border: A Social Study of Religion, Politics and Football in a North Wales Community* (London, 1957) contains a fascinating sociological study of the internal personal dynamics of a north Wales village club. Peter Corrigan, *100 Years of Welsh Soccer* (Cardiff, 1976) is a readable overview of the Welsh game. Ian Garland, *The History of the Welsh Cup, 1877–1993* (Wrexham, 1993) is detailed and useful. For biographies of Welsh players, again often considering what the players meant to the writers, see Huw Richards and Peter Stead (eds), *For Club and Country: Welsh Football Greats* (Cardiff, 2000). For the fans' view of Welsh football see Keith Haynes (ed.), *Come on Cymru* (Wilmslow, 1999) and Keith Haynes (ed.), *Come on Cymru 2000* (Wilmslow, 2000). Both collections are uneven and contentious but are passionate and entertaining nonetheless. There are numerous popular works on specific Welsh clubs, which can be found listed at my web-based *Bibliography of Football in Wales*: *www.staff.ucsm.ac.uk/ mjohnes/biblio.htm*. The best introduction to the academic history of football is Dave Russell, *Football and the English: A Social History of Association Football, 1863–1995* (Preston, 1997), a work that has huge relevance for anyone interested in Welsh football.

For a well-footnoted description of early sports and games in Wales see Hilarie M. Waddington, 'Games and athletics in bygone Wales, *Transactions of the Honourable Society of Cymmrodorion* (1953), 84–100. Gareth Williams, 'Sport and society in Glamorgan, 1780–1980', in Prys Morgan (ed.), *Glamorgan County History*, vol. vi (Cardiff, 1988) looks at south Wales and is reprinted with revisions in his *1905 and all that*. Emma Lile, 'Athletic Competition in pre-Industrial Wales, *c*.1066–*c*.1888' (M.Phil. thesis, University of Birmingham, 1994) also contains much useful information on pre-industrial sporting pastimes. Trefor M. Owen, *The Customs and Traditions of Wales* (Llandysul, [1959] 1994), has references to sports and games as part of wider traditional customs. Richard Suggett, 'Festivals and social structure in early modern Wales', *Past and Present*, 152 (August 1996), 79–112, is also important for a perceptive analysis of this wider culture of traditional festive customs. For contrasting analyses of traditional sports and games in England see R. W. Malcolmson, *Popular Recreations in English Society* (Cambridge, 1993) and Hugh Cunningham, *Leisure in the Industrial Revolution, c.1780–c.1880* (London, 1980).

On Welsh cricket the work of Andrew Hignell leads the way. His *A 'Favourit' Game: Cricket in South Wales before 1914* (Cardiff, 1992) is an excellent starting point, which usefully applies techniques from the discipline of geography to social history. Less academic, but still historically informed, is his *The History of Glamorgan CCC* (London, 1988). Hignell has also written two illuminating biographies of Welsh cricketers: *The Skipper: a Biography of Wilf Wooller* (Litlington, 1995) and *Maurice Turnbull: A Welsh Sporting Hero* (Stroud, 2001). For the wider history of cricket see Derek Birley, *A Social History of English Cricket* (London, 1999) and Jack Williams, *Cricket and England: A Cultural and Social History of the Inter-war Years* (London, 1999).

My analysis of Edwardian and inter-war Welsh boxers owes much to Dai Smith, 'Focal heroes: a Welsh fighting class', in Richard Holt (ed.), *Sport and the Working Class in Modern Britain* (Manchester, 1990), an essay reprinted in Smith's *Aneurin Bevan and the World of South Wales* (Cardiff, 1993). Bob Lonkhurst, *Man of Courage: The Life and Career of Tommy Farr* (Lewes, 1997) is an informative biography. Fred Deakin, *Welsh Warriors* (Stone, 1990) is a celebratory collection of short biographies of Welsh boxers. For the wider early history of boxing see Dennis Brailsford, *Bareknuckles: A Social History of Prize Fighting* (Cambridge, 1989). For the later history see Stan Shipley, 'Boxing', in Tony Mason (ed.), *Sport in Britain* (Cambridge, 1989). For academic work on equestrian and field sports see R. J. Moore-Colyer, 'Gentlemen, horses and the turf in nineteenth-century Wales', *Welsh History Review*, 16, 1 (1992), 47–62, and his 'Field Sports, conservation and the countryside in Georgian and Victorian Wales', *Welsh History Review*, 16, 3 (1993), 308–25. There is also much information in Brain Lee, *The Races Came Off: The Story of Point-to-Point Racing in South and West Wales, 1887–1935* (Cardiff, 1986). Mike Huggins, *Flat Racing and British Society, 1790–1914: A Social and Economic History* (London, 2000) and Roger Munting, *Hedges and Ditches: A Social and Economic History of National Hunt Racing* are important wider studies of horse racing.

R. Merfyn Jones, 'The mountaineering of Wales, 1880–1925', *Welsh History Review*, 19, 1 (June 1998), 44–67, is an illuminating study of a rural sport. Martin Johnes, 'Poor man's cricket: baseball, class and community in south Wales, *c*.1880–1950', *International Journal of the History of Sport*, 17, 4 (December 2000), 153–66, meanwhile explores an urban sport within its wider social context. E. J. Thomas, 'The history of physical education in Wales to 1970' (M.Ed. thesis, University of Manchester, 1979) looks at a range of sources for different school sports. Lynn Hughes, *Pendine Races: Motor Racing over Fifty Years* (Llandysul, 2000) is a fascinating if somewhat too detailed account. Wyn Williams (ed.), *Sport in Wales* (Denbigh, 1958) is a mixed but useful collection of contemporary writing and is especially valuable for less prominent Welsh sports. Albert Baker, *The History of Quoits in Wales: International and Individual Records* (Abertillery, 1949) is informative on this popular but marginalized sport. For academic work on the origins of athletics see Emma Lile, 'Professional pedestrianism in south Wales during the nineteenth century', *The Sports Historian*, 20, 2 (November 2000), 94–105. John Collins, Alan and Brenda Currie, Mike Walters and Clive Williams, *The History of Welsh Athletics* (Llanelli, 2002) contains much excellent information but is rather unfocussed. Brain Lee, *The Great Welsh Sprint: The Story of the Welsh Powderhall Handicap, 1903–34* (Pontypridd, 1999) is nostalgic but useful.

Women's sport in Wales has received little attention. Emma Lile, 'Women and sport in Aberystwyth, 1870–1914' (MA thesis, University of Wales, 1995) contains a wealth of information from west Wales. There is a section on women's football in Martin Johnes, *Soccer and Society: South Wales, 1900–39* (Cardiff, 2002). For the wider history of women in modern Wales see Deirdre Beddoe, *Out of the Shadows: A History of Women in Twentieth-Century Wales* (Cardiff, 2000). More sociological than historical but key nonetheless for the wider history of women's sport is Jennifer Hargreaves, *Sporting Females: Critical Issues in the History and Sociology of Women's Sport* (London, 1994).

Literature has much potential as a contemporary source for sport. For a stimulating review of the relevant Welsh material see Gareth Williams, 'Postponing death: sport and literature in Wales', *New Welsh Review*, 36 (Spring 1997), 37–46 (revised version published as 'The dramatic turbulence of some irrecoverable football game: sport, literature and Welsh identity', in Grant Jarvie (ed.), *Sport in the Making of Celtic Cultures* (London, 1999)). Perhaps the two most vivid and enjoyable Welsh novels that contain much on sport are Jack Jones, *Rhondda Roundabout* (London, 1934) and Ron Berry, *The Full-Time Amateur* (London, 1966). The classic but heavily romanticized Richard Llewelyn, *How Green was my Valley* (London, 1939) has a description of a rugby international. For a grittier, more recent view of rugby and Welsh life see Lewis Davies, *Work, Sex and Rugby* (London, 1993).

Wider accounts of leisure in Wales are unusual but important if the wider context of sport is to be understood. Peter Stead, 'Popular culture', in Trevor Herbert and Gareth Elwyn Jones (eds), *Post-War Wales* (Cardiff, 1995), pp. 107–32, offers a brief overview of the post-1945 period. Andy Croll, *Civilizing the Urban: Popular Culture and Public Space in Merthyr, c.1870–1914* (Cardiff, 2000) perceptively explores the contributions popular culture made (and did not make) to wider conceptions of civic pride and respectability. Gareth Williams, *Valleys of Song: Music and Society in Wales, 1840–1914* (Cardiff, 1998) is a vivid social history that centres on choral music. Stephen Ridgwell, 'South Wales cinema in the 1930s', *Welsh History Review*, 17, 4 (1995), 590–615 begins the history of Welsh cinema-going. Andy Croll and Martin Johnes, 'A heart of darkness? Leisure, respectability and the aesthetics of vice in Victorian Wales', in Mike Huggins and J. A. Mangan (eds), *Disreputable Pleasures? Less Virtuous Victorians at Play* (London, 2003) explores the shifting nature of notions of respectability in leisure.

For the wider history of Wales, John Davies, *A History of Wales* offers a magisterial tour. The essays in Gareth Elwyn Jones and Dai Smith (eds), *The People of Wales* (Llandysul, 1999) provide perceptive overviews. Kenneth O. Morgan, *Rebirth of a Nation: Wales, 1880–1980* (Cardiff/Oxford, 1981) is a seminal work that sees Wales as a society unified by a sense of nation. In contrast, the work of Dai Smith (notably *Aneurin Bevan and the World of South Wales* (Cardiff, 1993) and *Wales: A Question for History* (Bridgend, 1999) (a revised version of his *Wales! Wales?* (London, 1984)) places more emphasis on the wider unity of the British working class and the gulfs that existed between classes within Wales. There are a number of important studies of society in specific places. Chris Williams, *Capitalism, Community and Conflict: The South Wales Coalfield, 1898–1947* (Cardiff, 1998) is the best introduction to life in the coalfield, while his *Democratic Rhondda: Politics and Society, 1885–1951* (Cardiff, 1996) takes a more political perspective. Russell Davies, *Secret Sins: Sex, Violence and Society in Carmarthenshire, 1870–1920* (Cardiff, 1996) is a brilliant study that emphasises the experiences of ordinary individuals in a society that stood on the boundary between industry and agriculture. R. Merfyn Jones, *The North Wales Quarrymen, 1874–1922* (Cardiff, 1982), is another study that is both scholarly and highly readable. For the Welsh overseas see William D. Jones, *Wales in America: Scranton and the Welsh,*

1860–1920 (Cardiff, 1993), which acknowledges that sport was an aspect of Welsh culture that migrants consciously used to remain in touch with their roots.

For wider debates of Welsh identity, Neil Evans, 'Writing the social history of modern Wales: approaches, achievements and problems', *Social History*, 17, 3 (1992), 479–92, and R. Merfyn Jones, 'Beyond identity? The reconstruction of the Welsh', *Journal of British Studies*, 31 (1992), 330–57, both provide important contributions and useful introductions to the wider literature. For issues of identity in relation to sport, Martin Johnes 'Eighty minute patriots? National identity and sport in modern Wales', *International Journal of the History of Sport*, 17, 4 (2000), 93–110, is an earlier incarnation of some of the ideas presented here. Neil Evans and Paul O'Leary, 'Playing the game: sport and ethnic minorities in modern Wales', in Neil Evans, Paul O'Leary and Charlotte Williams (eds), *A Tolerant Nation? Exploring Ethnic Diversity in Wales* (Cardiff, 2003), tackles such issues in relation to Irish and black communities in Wales. Jeff Hill and Jack Williams, (eds), *Sport and Identity in the North of England* (Keele, 1996) is a thorough and highly illuminating study with much relevance for other regions. For an introduction to sport and national identity in Scotland that draws wider conclusions for the British 'Celtic fringe' see Grant Jarvie, 'Sport, nationalism and cultural identity', in Lincoln Allison (ed.), *The Changing Politics of Sport* (Manchester, 1993). Also see Grant Jarvie and Graham Walker (eds), *Scottish Sport and the Making of the Nation: Ninety Minute Patriots?* (Leicester, 1994).

The classic academic overview of the social history of British sport (with due attention to Wales) is Richard Holt, *Sport and the British: A Modern History* (Oxford, 1989). Derek Birley's trilogy, *Sport and the Making of Britain* (Manchester, 1993); *Land of Sport and Glory: Sport and British Society, 1887–1910* (Manchester, 1995); and *Playing the Game: Sport and British Society, 1910–45* (Manchester, 1995) also contains a wealth of information that does not ignore Wales, although it lacks the overall focus of Holt's survey. Neil Tranter, *Sport, Economy and Society in Britain, 1750–1914* (Cambridge, 1998) succinctly but perceptively introduces the relevant debates and literature for its period. Wray Vamplew, *Pay Up and Play the Game: Professional Sport in Britain,*

1875–1914 (Cambridge, 1988) is an important examination of financial aspects of sport. John Lowerson, *Sport and the English Middle Class, 1870–1914* (Manchester, 1995) comprehensively explores the often over-looked middle-class involvement in sport. The inter-war period still awaits its definitive overview but Stephen G. Jones, *Workers at Play: A Social and Economic History of Leisure, 1918–1939* (London, 1986) is a good starting point. Ross McKibbin, *Classes and Cultures: England 1918–1951* (Oxford, 1998) devotes a useful chapter to sport. For the post-1945 years there are two excellent texts that both include sections on Wales: Martin Polley, *Moving the Goalposts: A History of Sport and Society since 1945* (London, 1998) and Richard Holt and Tony Mason, *Sport in Britain, 1945–2000* (Oxford, 2000). For introductions to the sociology of sport see Ellis Cashmore, *Making Sense of Sport* (London, 3rd edn, 2000) and John Horne, Alan Tomlinson and Garry Whannel, *Understanding Sport: An Introduction to the Sociological and Cultural Analysis of Sport* (London, 1999). Raymond Boyle and Richard Haynes, *Power Play: Sport, the Media and Popular Culture* (Harlow, 2000) perceptively looks at the key theme of the media.

Finally, the bibliographic work of Richard W. Cox is key to any serious student of sports history, most notably: *British Sport: A Bibliography to 2000*, three volumes (London, 2002).

Index